Get Wealth

Get Wealth

God's Inherent Power To Make You A Covenant Broker

Frederick Osei-Manu

Copyright 2018—Frederick Osei-Manu

All rights reserved. This book is protected by the copyright laws of Ghana. This book may not be copied or reprinted for commercial gain or profit. The use of short quotations or occasional page copying for personal or group study is permitted and encouraged. Permission will be granted upon request. Scripture quotations are taken from the KING JAMES VERSION of the Bible, unless otherwise. Emphasis within Scripture is the author's.

For copies, contact
 Published by Menorah House Publication
 P. O. Box 17455, Accra
 Telephone or Text: 0233(0)244735485
 Email: fred18osei@hotmail.com

ISBN: 978-9988-2-7004-9

Editors: Charismata Editorial Services, Dr. (Mrs) Anita Akosua Osei Manu, Seth Odarkwei Lamptey, Mrs. Wilhelmina Asabea Asante-Asamani, Frederick Osei-Manu and Roland Bruce

Cover & Page Layout: Roland Bruce

Dedication

I dedicate this book to my sister, Doreen Yaa Ofosua Obeng. You have played such a vital role in my life and for this I am grateful. Thanks for all these years of being a wonderful person to me. Your love and contribution will never be forgotten in my world.

Acknowledgements

To the man who taught me the laws of money, my dad Seth Osei-Manu- I acknowledge you at this time in particular because if you had not tutored me early and well, I would not have come this far. So, I say thank you.

I want to also recognise Daniel Yeboah–Frimpong for paving a way for me when I needed it most during the course of writing this book. I appreciate your friendship which goes all the way back to childhood.

GET WEALTH   God's Inherent Power To Make You A Covenant Broker

x

Foreword

Right now, the economies of many nations across the globe are not in the best of shapes. Due to needless politics, greed, wars, wrong leadership, bad governance, among others, innocent citizens continue to struggle in poverty.

In many African countries, the gap between the rich and poor continues to widen. The ignorance of citizens is preyed upon by politicians to rape these struggling taxpayers. Notwithstanding the cyclical disappointments from these greedy politicians, electorates sadly continue to bank their hopes of economic freedom on them.

Unfortunately, a similar situation exists in the church. Greed for money has taken over the hearts of many believers, including some leaders. Pastors charge exorbitant fees before responding to invitations to preach the gospel. The rich are given special privileges while the poor are ignored. Some leaders deceive and extort money from unsuspecting believers. Pastors fight over members who are rich.

In 2014, a senior pastor cursed his associate pastor because the latter convinced one of the former's rich members to join his branch. Programs are organized in churches, not for the salvation and spiritual development of members, but for money to be acquired from them.

Families also pursue economic freedom. Women are encouraged to marry rich men and thereby relieve the families of financial hardship. A parent recently told one young man who wanted to marry her daughter, "Indeed, you are handsome. However, it takes more than being handsome to be able to afford clothes in a boutique." She chased the gentleman away because he was not rich. People continue to resort to mystical means of getting riches and wealth in order to impress society and be seen as relevant.

The world seems to be in a common pursuit—for money. The motives vary nonetheless. Some seek money to accomplish worthy causes, while others lust for it for vainglory. In some developed countries, employees work so hard for many hours, to be able to pay their bills and take care of other important needs.

Elsewhere, people kill and steal for money, to satisfy their lust for pleasure. How can you as a believer enjoy an economic advantage in these last days? How can you be prophetically positioned in these last days?

In this book, "GET WEALTH", the author unveils very profound and deep truth about wealth and possessing it the godly way. He insightfully uses the scriptures to draw the attention of the believer that we are living in the times when the Church must enjoy prophetic wealth. Time is running out, and soon Jesus shall return to rapture the Church.

It is, therefore, of critical importance that the body of Christ with a sense of urgency reaches out to get the unsaved converted and prepared for this great day. We cannot afford to watch the devil advance his cause and populate hell while we sleep. It is time for the church to arise and go get the unsaved converted. And this also requires money, as it oils the vehicle of the gospel. Every believer deserves to be wealthy—to advance the Kingdom of God. Get ready to be informed, inspired, empowered and equipped to be a statistic among the wealthy—as you journey through the propitious pages of this material.

Blessings and more.

Raphaelle Antwi,
Author, Founding President- Rain Foundations

Preface

Get Wealth is a must-read book for all who so desire to journey on the road to prosperity. God really wants the earth to be run by His sons. For far too long, most of the wealth and the business thereof in the earth have been in the hands of unbelievers and the systems of the world. Get Wealth seeks to throw light on how to regain those lost grounds. Note that taking over a territory demands wisdom and power on the part of the one doing so.

> WHEN A STRONG MAN, ARMED TO THE TEETH, STANDS GUARD IN HIS FRONT YARD, HIS PROPERTY IS SAFE AND SOUND. But what IF A STRONGER MAN COMES ALONG WITH SUPERIOR WEAPONS? THEN HE'S BEATEN AT HIS OWN GAME, THE ARSENAL THAT GAVE HIM SUCH CONFIDENCE HAULED OFF, AND HIS PRECIOUS POSSESSIONS PLUNDERED. (Luke 11:21–22) MSG.

The pages of this book will give you the knowledge to help you aim for your own expression as one God will use to take back what rightfully belongs to us. You are about to chart a new course in your life with this manuscript in your hands. Get Wealth will stretch your mind and challenge you to soar above your current reality. Remember this—we all came to earth with nothing but what we do with our lives here will determine whether we will be rich or poor.

It is true that I am writing about money, but at heart, I am writing about something far beyond money. Money has its place in life, not the vice versa, for life is bigger than money. Words that communicate life have been carefully chosen and interwoven with practical wisdom and knowledge to make you the reader benefit immensely on this journey of prosperity.

Get Wealth will spur you on to be all that God wants you to be concerning your finances. The wells of wealth have been dug right before your eyes but the responsibility is yours to fetch and to drink. Whether you fetch with a spoon, your hands, a cup or a bucket, the choice it left to you alone to make. Make a wise decision today in regard to your financial destiny.

In This Book

ACKNOWLEDGEMENTS .... **IX**
FOREWORD .... **XI**
PREFACE .... **XV**
    TRANSLATION INDEX xxi
        AN EXPLANATION OF ABBREVIATIONS .... *xxi*
    INTRODUCTION **01**
        WHAT IS THE ESSENCE OF THE POWER? 03
        YOUR PART IN ESTABLISHING THIS COVENANT 03

05 *chapter one*
    LIMITLESS POWER **05**

11 *chapter two*
    WISDOM: THE GATEWAY TO ALL RESOURCES **11**
        WISDOM AND HER CHILDREN 13
            1. Favour *14*
            2. Might In Words And Deeds *15*
            3. Achievements *16*
            4. Success *17*
            5. Better Days Ahead *17*
            6. Prominence *18*
            7. Defense *18*

21 *chapter three*
    SHIFT **21**
        FIVE COMMON WAYS BY WHICH SHIFTS OCCUR FINANCIALLY 24
            1. Personal Decision *24*
            2. Governmental Policies *25*
            3. Global Issues *25*
            4. Demonic Attacks *26*
            5. God's Interventions *27*

29 *chapter four*
    PROPHECY—YOUR WAY TO PROSPERITY **29**
        THE LION ROAR IS WORKING FOR ME 31
        I EXCEL FINANCIALLY 31
        I AM OVERFLOWING WITH WEALTH 32
        FAVOUR IN FINANCIAL MATTERS 32
        I AM ABOUNDING MORE AND MORE IN WEALTH 32
        I COME INTO A GOOD LAND 32
        I COME INTO EXCESSIVE WEALTH 33

35 chapter five
FIELD AND TREASURE 35
    LESSONS TO BE LEARNT 38

43 chapter six
ASPIRE 43
    SET YOUR FACE 47
    ELEVEN THINGS YOU HAVE TO ASPIRE TO IN LIFE 48
        1. To Gain A Good Education *48*
        2. To Own A Shop *48*
        3. Become A Giver or Philanthropist *48*
        4. To Own A Home *49*
        5. To Own A Car *50*
        6. To Have An Investment Portfolio *50*
        7. To Drink Well, Eat Well and Dress Well *50*
        8. To Have Good Relationships *50*
        9. To Be Planted In House of God *51*
        10. To Be A Soul Winner *52*
        11. To Have Friendship With God. *52*

55 chapter seven
THE POWER OF RESERVES 55

59 chapter eight
ACCEPTANCE OF THE ANOINTED ONES AND THE PROPHETS 59

65 chapter nine
MERCHANT GRACE 65
    TIME 67
    WISE USE OF MONEY 67
    BUY CHEAP AND SELL WITH A MARGIN 68
    DEALS 68
    THE ART OF SEEKING 68
    BUSINESS SENSE 69
    CAPACITY FOR STOREHOUSES 69
    ROUTES 70
    VARIETY 71

73 chapter ten
RELEASING YOUR NETS FOR A BREAKTHROUGH 73
    Eight Principles For Financial Breakthroughs 75
        1. Failure *75*
        2. You Need An Encourager / Inspirer *76*
        3. Make Use Of Your Kits / Expertise *76*
        4. Step Into The Deep *76*

- 5. You Are Surrounded By Miracles 76
- 6. You Need Helpers / Partners 77
- 7. Work With Others Cheerfully 77
- 8. Crazy Instruction 77

79 chapter eleven
BLESSINGS OF THE PATRIARCHS 79

89 chapter twelve
THE BEST OF THE LAND 89

93 chapter thirteen
NOTABLE GIVING 93
- The Churches in Macedonia 94
- Noah's Offering 96
- King Solomon's Building Of The Temple 96
- Cornelius A Man Of Giving 97
- The Widow's Two Mites 99
- Cake For Elijah 100
- Giving That Took Place At The Apostles' Feet 102
- The People Brought Too Much In Moses' Days 104

107 chapter fourteen
WITH OR WITHOUT MONEY 107
MISCONCEPTIONS ABOUT MONEY 109
- 1. Money Is The Root Of All Evil 109
- 2. Money Is For A Favoured Few 110
- 3. Money Is A Respecter Of Age, Gender, Certain Places And Education 110
- 4. Stolen Wealth Is Sweet 111
- 5. Those Who Hoard Money Have More Of It 111
- 6. Let Use Money Anyhow For Tomorrow We Will Make More 111

THINGS YOU MUST PLACE ABOVE MONEY 112
- 1. God 112
- 2. A Good Name 113
- 3. Family, Friendship & People 114
- 4. Character & Values 114
- 5. Your Position & Your Office 115
- 6. Loyalty 115
- 7. Life 117
- 8. Environment 118
- 9. Attending Church & Spiritual Things 119
- 10. The Future 119

121 chapter fifteen
COVENANT BROKERS... **121**
    TITHE AND OFFERING 123
    PRAISE 123
    GOOD HARVESTERS 124

127 chapter sixteen
BREAKING THE CYCLES OF POVERTY **127**
    ARE YOU SURVIVING OR LIVING? 130
    JUDGEMENT FOR THE RELEASE OF WEALTH 132
    MEGA RESTORATION 133

135 chapter seventeen
THE LEGACY **135**
    PEOPLE IN THE OLD TESTAMENT 137
        Abel *137*
        Noah *137*
        Abraham *138*
        David *139*
        Solomon *139*
    PEOPLE IN THE NEW TESTAMENT 140
        Wise Men *140*
        Jesus *140*
        Peter *140*
        Barnabas *141*
        Lydia *141*
    MODERN DAY 141

CONCLUSION 145

TRANSLATION INDEX

The author of this manuscript believes that the reading of the Bible from multiple translations helps one to get a firm understanding of scriptures. It also makes it easy for one to convey his or her ideas in a unique way. The author encourages the reader to actively collect more Bible translations to help the reader's walk with God.

AN EXPLANATION OF ABBREVIATIONS

The translations used in this manuscript can be identified by the following codes:

- **AMP**–Amplified Bible
- **AUV**–An Understandable Version
- **BBE**–Bible In Basic English
- **CEV**–Contemporary English Version
- **ERV**–Easy-to- Read Version
- **HCSB**–Holman Christian Standard Bible
- **JMNT**–Jonathan Mitchell New Testament
- **KJV**–King James Version
- **MOF**–James Moffatt Translation
- **MSG**–The Message
- **NET**–New English Translation
- **NIV**–New Living Version
- **NKJV**–New King James Version
- **NLV**–New Life Version
- **NRSV**–New Revised Standard Version
- **NSB**–New Simplified Bible
- **PHILLIPS**–J.B. Phillips New Testament
- **RSV**–Revised Standard Version
- **TLB**–The Living Bible
- **VOICE**–The Voice
- **WYC**–Wycliffe Bible

Introduction

This book is simply based on Deuteronomy 8:18 which reads: And you shall remember the LORD your God, for it is He who gives you POWER TO GET WEALTH, that He may establish His covenant which He swore to your fathers, as it is this day.

There is a saying that 'if you think education is expensive then try *ignorance*.' With this in mind, I say to you that if you think prosperity is a luxury and for a few, then you better try poverty. Tell me what poverty has achieved and I will be the first to tell you that it has robbed people, families and nations of what they could have become.

Why do we have people migrating from different blocks of Africa, Asia and South America in search of greener pastures in parts of Europe and United States of America? It is one thing and one thing only that drives these people: they are tired and fed up with poverty.

As much as we create a difference in our finances as to the choices we make, whether to sow or to hold back the seeds in our hands, it cannot be compared to the significant difference the LORD makes. In reality, we as men make a difference. Let us look at these:

- » "the measure" of giving out.
- » "the measure" of getting back.

Men have an element to play in it. What interests me the most is the person who moves men to give into our bosom? The simple answer is that it is the LORD.

> *...remember THE LORD THY GOD: for it is he that giveth thee power to get (Deuteronomy 8:18).*

> *Give, and [gifts] will be given to you; GOOD MEASURE, PRESSED DOWN, SHAKEN TOGETHER, and RUNNING OVER, WILL THEY POUR INTO [THE POUCH FORMED BY] THE BOSOM [OF YOUR ROBE AND USED AS A BAG]. For with the measure you deal out [with the measure you use when you confer benefits on others], IT WILL BE MEASURED BACK TO YOU. (Luke 6:38) AMP.*

From another perspective, the power to have seeds belongs to Him (God). He is indeed the rightful owner of all things. The power in the seed that unlocks the harvest belongs to Him. So then, if you are going to enjoy a successful journey of prosperity, then you must acknowledge His place in your life and world. The scripture below says it all:

> *PRAISE THE LORD, MY SOUL; ALL MY INMOST BEING, PRAISE HIS HOLY NAME. Praise the LORD, my soul, and FORGET NOT ALL HIS BENEFITS— who forgives all your sins and heals all your diseases, who redeems your life from the pit and crowns you with love and compassion, WHO SATISFIES YOUR DESIRES WITH GOOD THINGS SO THAT YOUR YOUTH IS RENEWED LIKE THE EAGLE. (Psalms 103:1-5) NIV.*

Therefore, the LORD'S input is of greater significance than others. Remember Him daily and give credit to Him.

WHAT IS THE ESSENCE OF THE POWER?

When I was young, I told the people around me that when I become rich, I would get myself a good car and a mansion to live in. This ambition is common among men. However, when I was schooled in the things of God, I realized that first and foremost, the wealth God brings into my life is for me to establish His covenant here on earth.

Establishing God's Kingdom and not mine is the focal point for this financial power. When we miss this, we are out of the tracks of true prosperity. Therefore, my money and yours are for God and His activities.

YOUR PART IN ESTABLISHING THIS COVENANT

God made a covenant with Abraham and said expressly to him—*Now the Lord had said unto Abram, Get thee out of thy country, and from thy kindred, and from thy father's house, UNTO A LAND THAT I WILL SHEW THEE: And I will make of thee a great nation, and I will bless thee, and make thy name great; and thou shalt BE A BLESSING: And I will bless them that bless thee, and curse him that curseth thee: and in thee shall all families of the earth be blessed. (Genesis 12:1–3).*

The whole idea of God getting wealth into your hands is simply so that the entire world (human race) will be blessed. Therefore on your part, you must make a decision to be a blessing to the men that come your way. Moreover, by this power, we can take lands and make them become our LORD's and of his CHRIST.

Those who dwell in our lands (i.e. be it schools, businesses, hotels, restaurants), *we can easily influence and impart the gospel of Christ to them.* God is at work in you and me to get back His estate (land). I hear this word in my spirit: the earth is my estate says the Lord.

In this estate, there my people dwell. My portion is my people. What is this portion? Worship is the portion. God is after men to get His worship. Your tithe and giving is also part of your worship. I have figured out that the use of money is a principal part of our worship of God. This explains why satan is after your money.

CHAPTER ONE

Limitless Power

Dreams and visions in the heart of many have gone unfulfilled because they were or are limited in the area of finance. Why stay unfulfilled, frustrated and worn out when there is power available for you to overcome every obstacle in this life?

---

*I*t is in my quest to find the secret that would allow men to live a life over and above frustration that I began to write this manuscript. Guess what will happen if you are limitless (unlimited, boundless, unrestrained) concerning your finances.

You can boldly come to the house of God without empty hands. You can afford to buy a house with smiles on your face. You can get a good education of your choice. You can easily move around and about in your own car. You can reach out to bless others without seething in the process. You can have a pretty tall list of things to do and have them accomplished when you are limitless.

The good news is that "there is a limitless power of God for all and sundry to get wealth." It is yours for the taking; so go for it. Deuteronomy 8:18 says it all—But thou shalt remember the LORD thy GOD: for it is he that giveth thee the power to get wealth, that he may establish his covenant which he sware unto thy fathers, as it is this day.

I live in a nation where now and then there is load shedding of power (electricity). This affects the productivity of business and also has a negative impact on the domestic life of its people. Therefore, the bottom line is this: where there is no power, there is no growth or progression. This truth applies both to physical and spiritual things.

To this day, I do not know any man who made an impact in history without the element of power. I am about to make a statement that will shock you to the core of your being "even God cannot rule this universe without power." That is why in the Lord's Prayer, there is this phrase—for yours [God] is the kingdom, power and the glory forever. Amen. (Matthew 6:13b).

> The LORD says, "I will make my people strong with power from me. They will go wherever they wish and wherever they go, they will be under my personal care. (Zechariah 10:12) TLB.

Under God's personal care, we are in no way limited. Limitation is not part of our diction or vocabulary. We can afford to go to the nations because we have God's backing to do so. I tend to like the expression "they will go wherever they wish."

This backing includes financial provision, safety and protection for the human lives on the mission field. We can also trust God to make His healing, saving, delivering power available to transform lives and societies we come in touch with.

Be it that you are in business or any other venture, you can break into new frontiers if you so wish because His word to you is I give you the power to make you strong than ever. Being financially strong is essential in this day and age when there is the economic crunch of the nations.

At present, there are many of God's people who are financially weak and barely living life, not to the fullest. A lot are under shoelace budgets thereby making it extremely difficult for them to give towards any Kingdom project. It is amazing to realise that if anything crosses their budget plans, their finances will be thrown into turmoil.

I know a thing or two about God's power: it can give one strength, a voice and influence in any environment. This is why I recommend God's unlimited, unending power to you. Seek to connect to His power and also come under his personal care—that is an amazing place to be.

Moreover, this limitless power can make you soar financially like an eagle while others chicken out about their financial state. I like how this verse of scripture brings it out.

> *He [God] giveth power to the faint; and to them that have no might he increaseth strength. Even the youths shall faint and be weary, and the young men shall utterly fall: But they that wait upon the Lord shall renew their strength; they shall mount up with wings as eagles; they shall run, and not be weary; and they shall walk, and not faint. (Isaiah 40:29–31).*

> *For this purpose I have raised you up, that I may show MY POWER in you and that my name may be declared in all the earth. (Romans 9:17).*

Power is when we are raised up to manifest what God can do in us and through us. Power is what changes the course of history in the Earth. Power is what turns the poor to become rich. Your declaration of wealth must be by power. Anything less will prevent you to manifesting financially because the force of opposition is great.

Power is what gives you a say in God's economy and the economy of the earth. Power to become rich is not farfetched.

John 1:12 beautifully puts it—*But as many as RECEIVED HIM, to them he gave power to the sons of God, even to them that believe in his name.*

This power is available and it is in your ability to receive and believe that puts you in the place of power. The power to love, the power to share, the power to be rich, the power to forgive and much more are all inclusive in God's divine power.

For me, I have purposed with determination to be part of the people God will raise with the power to get wealth, who will shamelessly declare His goodness to men. I cannot imagine a day living without the power of God flowing in and through me.

Among the many reasons why you were born is for God to showcase you as His to the world that He is behind your success for your being rich. Do I need to say something that will stay with you for the rest of your life? This will be the one thing— "God has raised men from nowhere, men without credentials and men without beautiful backgrounds He has raised to become somebodies." Time and space will not allow me to enumerate but believe me, it is really a tall list. From A to Z, God has single-handedly raised people to prominence.

Let us take a look at what Luke 1:49 has to say—*For he that is mighty hath done to me great things; and holy is his name.* Remember God has you on his mind to do great things in your life and with your life if only you will allow Him room to do what He alone does best with men.

CHAPTER TWO

Wisdom: The Gateway to All Resources

> *When it comes to prosperity, people, in general, have a mind of their own as to how it should look and be experienced. Many have reduced prosperity to the ability to gain things. It is especially in this generation that many have become "material and things oriented" people.*

*I*n my search to know the truth about prosperity, I have found out that wisdom is the principal thing we should aspire to gain it. Wisdom is a Person, a Spirit and a Gift all in one—Jesus. With this insight, your quest and passion in life should be for wisdom.

Wisdom is what gives birth to things. Many things are at the beck and call of wisdom. Now read the scripture below with an eagle eye:

The Lord brought me forth as the first of his works, before his deeds of old; I was formed long ages ago, at the very beginning, when the world came to be. When there were no watery depths, I was given birth, when there were no springs overflowing with water; before the mountains were settled in place, before the hills, I was given birth, before he made the world or its fields or any of the dust of the earth. I was there when he set the heavens in place, when he marked out the horizon on the face of the deep, when he established the clouds above and fixed securely the fountains of the deep, when he gave the sea its boundary so that the waters would not overstep his command, and when he marked out the foundations of the earth. Then I was constantly at his side. I was filled with delight day after day, rejoicing always in his presence, rejoicing in his whole world and delighting in the human race. (Proverbs 8:22–31).

What did you see? I believe you were dazed to see that wisdom was the springboard for things to make their way into our world. Note that God in His own capacity as the Creator of all things was in perfect union with wisdom before things came into existence.

Wisdom was responsible for these ten (10) things, enumerated below:

- » Watery depths
- » Springs that overflows with water
- » Mountains and hills settled in their place
- » World, fields and dust
- » Set heavens in place
- » Marked the horizon of the face of the deep
- » Established the clouds above
- » Fixed securely the fountains of the deep
- » Gave the sea its boundary
- » Marked the foundations of the earth

WISDOM AND HER CHILDREN

...But wisdom is justified of her children (Matthew 11:19). Wisdom has many children. The children of wisdom are very prominent and they have a right to be heard everywhere they are. There is nobody in life that can do without children of wisdom in the gates of society. Of a truth, anybody who decides to not relate with wisdom is heading for a fall.

Let me quickly introduce you to the children of wisdom. Here, I will try to just mention a few for our study.

1. Favour

In my opinion, after breath, wisdom is one of an essential commodity for man to live the full life God intended for him here on earth. In Acts 7:10, I found out that favour coupled with wisdom was what gave Joseph a place in the sight of Pharaoh, the King of Egypt. We are not talking about any ordinary man but a King who in ancient times was revered and considered the most powerful man to rule nearly all the civilized nations in the world.

This King found something special in Joseph, for which reason he made him a Governor over the whole realm of Egypt and over all the houses in the land. What really fascinates me is that Joseph started life at age 17 as a slave in Egypt. We all know that a slave is one who has no reputation and substance to his or her name.

So for Joseph, to start life with nothing and down the line to have the whole land before him is really pretty amazing. What I am trying to bring out for you to notice is that in life, you may start with nothing but there lies a whole world of possibilities for you to someday have what you want.

Get this in your heart—good things gravitate towards wisdom. You tell me Joseph could not have been second to Pharaoh in a land where he was a stranger if his wisdom had not been sought for.

Moreover, it is this same wisdom that made Joseph advise his siblings to tell Pharaoh that they were nomads (shepherds) if they asked about their occupation. This advice looked normal because the family was already into livestock rearing. But there was more to it in that the best part of the land "Goshen" was on offer for them to dwell in. Now, they could do what they knew how to do best in Egypt; if they answered rightly. We, therefore, can say that wisdom was what gave Israel the best part of Egypt upon their arrival into the land.

2. Might In Words And Deeds

> *And Moses was LEARNED IN ALL THE WISDOM OF EGYPTIANS, and was MIGHTY IN WORDS and IN DEEDS. (Acts 7:22).*

There is the wisdom of God and there is the wisdom of the world and the wisdom of Egypt is an example of the latter. You and I know that the wisdom of God surpasses all the wisdom of nations put together. For the weakness of God is stronger than the strength of men and His foolishness wiser than the wisdom of men.

So then, if Moses could do mighty exploits in words and in deeds, then consider how much he would do with the wisdom of God. Later, you will discover from the book of Exodus that Moses did far better and more miracles than any man in his generation because the spirit of wisdom was at work in him.

Today, people are travelling all over the earth to learn and also gain wisdom from various universities in the nations. This should tell you how much great value is placed on wisdom. How rich are you in words and deeds? We are talking about words that touch lives. Words that inspire and bring hope to many. Do you have words that encourage and drive people to attain success? Do you carry and speak words that creation pays attention to? Your righteous deeds must begin to speak in the streets, gates, homes and virtually everywhere.

3. Achievements

> *Then Solomon BUILT HIS OWN PALACE, which took THIRTEEN YEARS TO CONSTRUCT ...these buildings were constructed ENTIRELY HUGE, EXPENSIVE STONES, CUT TO MEASURE. (1 Kings 7:1,9) TLB.*

The palace which Solomon built in his days was one that was outstanding for the rooms in this palace were not like anything seen before it:

- » One of the rooms is called Hall of the Forest of Lebanon [measuring 150ft long, 75ft wide and 45ft high]. (See 1 Kings 7:2)
- » Another room is called Hall of Pillars [measuring 75ft long, 45ft wide, with a porch covered with a canopy which was supported by pillars]. (See 1 Kings 7:6)
- » Others rooms were the Throne Room / Judgement Hall [the place where Solomon listened to legal matters]. (See 1 Kings 7:7)
- » The courtyard behind the Throne Room (See 1Kings 7:8).

All these works were done by skilled men and done with a touch of class and excellence.

4. Success

> *If the axe is dull and the man does not whet the edge, he must put forth more strength, but WISDOM HELPS HIM TO SUCCEED. (Ecclesiastes 10:10) AMP.*

Wisdom makes you succeed with 'sweatless' effort. It takes wisdom for you to exert less strength for a greater result. A man without wisdom will apply more strength to hew a tree and if care is not taken, the axe head will fly into his face to his own hurt.

Wisdom, on the other hand, will preserve the life of a worker and keep his tools in good shape. The time spent to weigh matters (brainstorm) before execution is better than rushing to implement ideas without first taking thoughts. Wisdom cuts away loss and maximizes profit. Wisdom, therefore, will make you sharpen your abilities for financial victories.

5. Better Days Ahead

> *Do not say, why were the old days better than these? For it is not wise or because of wisdom that you ask this. (Ecclesiastes7: 10) AMP.*

Wisdom is what awakens imagination and imagination is what brings the future into perspective. Many are trapped with the saying "the good old days." They will refer you to how business thrived and the systems in which they lived favoured them in the past. Unfortunately for these people, those days are gone and cannot be lived in again.

So then, wisdom demands that we look forward to better days ahead. Wisdom proposes that there is more money to be made today and tomorrow than yesterday. Indeed, there are more opportunities ahead than ever were before.

6. Prominence

> *Who is like the wise man? And who knows the interpretation of a thing? A man's WISDOM MAKES HIS FACE SHINE, and the hardness of his countenance is changed. (Ecclesiastes 8:1) AMP.*

To shine is to be prominent in an area. Almost all who have come into financial prominence have done so by wisdom. The right interpretation of things (facts, figures and patterns) is essential in any enterprise. The man whose face shines is one with a brilliant intellectual power. Wisdom makes a man shine in his thought, speech and makes people take note of them.

The difference between financial glory and financial crunch is dependent on the right application of wisdom. By wisdom, your financial seasons can change. When wisdom comes in contact with hardness, it makes it soft. Wisdom has the potency to make life easy for you; so let wisdom reign in your endeavours.

7. Defense

> *For WISDOM IS A DEFENSE even as money is a defense, but the excellency of knowledge is that wisdom shields and preserves the life of him who has it. (Ecclesiastes 7:12) AMP.*

Just as money can provide a safety cushion to those who have it; so can wisdom also formulate policies and plans to ward off leakages in your financial setup. Wisdom has the power to turn trash into money; this in itself is a defence.

Wisdom will tell you to buy plenty during a boom to save against a lean season. Wisdom will stop you from wasting your life on useless ventures. Wisdom provides higher guidance than even financial experts can provide.

CHAPTER THREE

SHIFT

> *Currently, the earth is undergoing a wholesale shift. The shift is taking place outside the church environment as well as within the church. This shift will undoubtedly reflect in the economies of nations and people all over the world.*

A shift is like moving from one end of the pendulum to the other end within a blink of the eye. There is a shift and acceleration ongoing in the Kingdom of God. The old is giving way to the new. We are at the edge of moving from faith to faith and from glory to glory.

As God initiates this new movement in our world, we should position ourselves with a new paradigm shift in our mentality to be able to preserve what God is doing in the now. If we fail to discern this new move of God, we will be trapped behind curtains of the old.

Note—this generation is looking for new direction for a new work. The search is on for "new wine in new wineskin" messages. It is, therefore, important to flow with the new heavenly sound concerning finances. A shift from little to plenty, few to many, lack to abundance and from more to more than you can carry will characterise this current move of God concerning finances.

Now watch what the scripture says in Luke 16:16—*THE LAW and THE PROPHETS WERE UNTIL JOHN: since that time the Kingdom of God is preached, and every man presseth into it.* The law and the prophets represent one era and the Kingdom of God also signifies another era entirely. The preaching and teachings that have the Kingdom of God as their central theme provide a higher radical shift of God's way of doing things to its hearers.

There is a vista in Luke 16:16 that allows us to press into God beyond the patriarchs and the prophets of old. The level of wealth exhibited in the old cannot be compared to what God has for His people in the new and now. The world is about to see a new dimension of riches God is about to pour into the life of believers.

Someone may be saying I am overstretching the revelation and application of this scripture. You would notice that when one is in the "thousand flow" and you start to talk about the "million flow" not even about the "billion flow"; there is the likelihood they will not embrace your message. Why- because this particular message does not fit into their reality. Remember this truth, those who have tasted the old do not desire the new.

Then He spoke a parable to them: "No one puts a piece from a new garment on an old one; otherwise the new makes a tear, and also the piece that was taken out of the new does not match the old. And no one puts new wine into old wineskins; or else the new wine will burst the wineskins and be spilled, and the wineskins will be ruined. But new wine must be put into new wineskins, and both are preserved. AND NO ONE, HAVING DRUNK OLD WINE, IMMEDIATELY DESIRES NEW; FOR HE SAYS, 'THE OLD IS BETTER.'" (Luke 5:36-39) NKJV.

Moreover, I have found out that "those who ask not, receive not. Those who ask receive. So allow those of us who are dreamers to dream with God concerning the ongoing shift in the realm of finances."

> *For I will look on you favourably and make you fruitful, multiply you and confirm My covenant with you. (Leviticus 26:9) NKJV.*

It is interesting to note how God emphatically instructed the people of Israel to clear out the old to make way for the new. That is a shift right there. The old has no choice but to make way for the new. The new is always better than the old in God's dealings with men.

In years past, God confirmed His unbreakable covenant with Israel by making them extremely fruitful and multiplying their number as well as their influence on the earth. I am a firm believer we have entered into a time and age in God where we will experience some of the strange acts of His favour. The covenant of blessing will work profusely for you and it will ignite a divine shift in your life.

FIVE COMMON WAYS BY WHICH SHIFTS OCCUR FINANCIALLY

1. Personal Decision

The financial decisions you make will decide whether you become rich or poor. Often, we blame others for our financial woes. To be frank with you, whether money moves to you or away from is based on your decisions.

> *He who has a slack hand becomes poor, but the hand of the diligent makes rich. He who gathers in summer is a wise son; He who sleeps in harvest is a son who causes shame. (Proverbs 10:4,5) NKJV.*

2. Governmental Policies

We do not live in isolation in the world. Directly or indirectly, governmental policies go a long way to affecting us positively or negatively. These policies can determine how much a loaf of bread should cost, what you pay towards a road levy, what kind of goods you can import or export, etc.

I remember my father told me of a time in the history of Ghana when the government asked its citizens to change their capital with the banks because they wanted to implement the redenomination of the Cedi. Those who did were safe but those who were afraid to do so because of the ongoing revolution lost their financial position in a day.

> *Jesus said, "YOU'RE TIED DOWN TO THE MUNDANE [government policies]; I'm in touch with what is beyond your horizons. YOU LIVE IN TERMS OF WHAT YOU SEE AND TOUCH. I'm living on other terms. (John 8:23, the writer's addition) MSG.*

3. Global Issues

> *The famine was over all the face of the earth [globe]... (Genesis 41:56) NKJV.*

We have found out with time that what impacts one nation can have a ripple effect on other nations and even the globe as a whole. Indeed, we live in a more globalised village than any generation in history. Naturally speaking, I can say that global issues have a say on how big your pocket or purse is.

4. Demonic Attacks

> *And a messenger came to Job and said, "The oxen were plowing and the donkeys feeding beside them, when the Sabeans raided them and took them away—indeed they have killed the servants with the edge of the sword; and I alone have escaped to tell you!" While he was still speaking, another also came and said, "The fire of God fell from heaven and burned up the sheep and the servants, and consumed them; and I alone have escaped to tell you!" While he was still speaking, another also came and said, "The Chaldeans formed three bands, raided the camels and took them away, yes, and killed the servants with the edge of the sword; and I alone have escaped to tell you!" (Job 1:14–17) NKJV.*

In a day, Job lost all his wealth. From being the richest man in the East to become the poorest of the poor is really a tragedy. You ask yourself: "how come this happened to a righteous man?" Satan sought for permission from God before he could touch Job's wealth. This was done to see if Job would not curse God for his troubles.

The band of raiders that took Job's oxen, donkeys, camels and the fire that consumed his sheep were all Satan's ploy. I want you to know that Satan has no power to touch your substance if God does not allow him. God is the only One who has the final word about your finances. Do you know after all this tragedy God blessed Job twice as much as before?

And THE LORD RESTORED JOB'S LOSSES when he prayed for his friends. INDEED THE LORD GAVE JOB TWICE AS MUCH AS HE HAD BEFORE. Then all his brothers, all his sisters, and all those who had been his acquaintances before, came to him and ate food with him in his house; and they consoled him and comforted him for all the adversity that the Lord had brought upon him. Each one gave him a piece of silver and each a ring of gold. Now the Lord blessed the latter days of Job more than his beginning; for he had FOURTEEN THOUSAND SHEEP, SIX THOUSAND CAMELS, ONE THOUSAND YOKE OF OXEN, and ONE THOUSAND FEMALE DONKEYS. (Job 42:10–12) NKJV.

5. God's Interventions

He raises the poor out of the dust, And lifts the needy out of the ash heap, That He may seat him with princes—With the princes of His people. (Psalm 113:7-8) NKV.

God has a speciality in bringing about an economic shift in the lives of people. He picks men and women of no repute and makes them sit in places of honour. When God makes up his mind to elevate a person, there is actually no limit to how far this person can go. He indeed makes one become a thousand in a record time. *A little one shall become a thousand, And a small one a strong nation. I, THE LORD, WILL HASTEN IT IN ITS TIME." (Isaiah 60:22) NKJV.*

CHAPTER FOUR

Prophecy— Your Way To Prosperity

> *I will pour out my Spirit IN THOSE DAYS. AND THEY SHALL PROPHESY. (Acts 2:18).*

Prophecy is simply an inspired word or a prophetic word breathed on by God to the believer for him or her to speak forth that word into the earth to cause changes. Irrefutably, prophecy is all about confession. Confessing what God has said is prophecy.

> *Having then gifts differing according to the grace that is given to us, let us use them: IF PROPHECY, LET US PROPHESY IN PROPORTION TO OUR FAITH. (Romans 12:6).*

In this glorious age of the church, God's people will certainly have an urge to prophesy wealth into their circles to enable the Church to accomplish the Great Commission.

These groups of people will prophesy on the mountain tops, in the valleys, in their houses, closets, streets and marketplaces that "Money Cometh". What has prophecy got to do with money? It has everything to do with it. Since money has wings, it will fly on the winds of prophecy.

Everything that exists on the earth came forth out of the voice of God and, therefore, will certainly hearken to it. Vegetation came forth out of the voice of God. Money which is a product of vegetation has no other choice but to move in the direction of the voice of God's people.

> *… THE WORD IS NIGH THEE, even IN THY MOUTH, and IN THY HEART: that is, THE WORD OF FAITH, which we preach. (Romans 10:9).*

The preaching of the word of faith is what opens men to the world of prosperity. Hearing alone is not enough, speaking the word of faith and making bold prosperity declarations backed with a lifestyle of giving are essential for one to enjoy the full package of prosperity. The word is near you.

The words that can make all the difference are stored up in your heart waiting for the time your mouth will release the blessing thereof. Till your mouth aligns with your heart concerning prosperity and for that matter anything in the Kingdom of God, prosperity will be like a mirage to you.

In this chapter, I will attempt to bring to your attention a few scriptures you can use to release your wealth. Below is a list of them:

THE LION ROAR IS WORKING FOR ME

> *THE LION HAS ROARED; who will not fear? THE LORD GOD HAS SPOKEN; who can but prophesy? (Amos 3:8).*

Jesus the Lion of Judah has roared for the full release of your wealth. So the enemy has no choice but to take his hands of your wealth. God has already spoken about your financial destiny, in that it is glorious. Therefore, go out there to claim your portion.

I EXCEL FINANCIALLY

> *Now as you excel in everything—in faith, in speech, in knowledge, in utmost eagerness, and in our love for you—so we want you to EXCEL ALSO IN THIS GENEROUS UNDERTAKING. (2 Corinthians 8:7) NRSV.*

Say to yourself: as I excel in my giving, I also excel in receiving my harvest. Declare that your harvest is looking for you everywhere.

I AM OVERFLOWING WITH WEALTH

PROSPERITY SHALL OVERFLOW Jerusalem LIKE A RIVER, SAYS THE LORD, for I will send it; THE RICHES OF THE GENTILES WILL FLOW TO HER (Isaiah 66:12a) TLB.

FAVOUR IN FINANCIAL MATTERS

For they did not gain possession of the land by their own sword, nor did their own arm save them: but it was Your right hand, Your arm, and the light of Your countenance, BECAUSE YOU FAVOURED THEM. You are my King, O God; COMMAND VICTORIES FOR JACOB. (Psalms 44:3,4) NKJV.

I AM ABOUNDING MORE AND MORE IN WEALTH

Finally then, brethren, we urge and exhort in the Lord Jesus that you should ABOUND MORE AND MORE, just as you received from us how you ought to walk and to please God. (1Thessalonians 4:1) NKJV.

I COME INTO A GOOD LAND

FOR THE LORD YOUR GOD IS BRINGING YOU INTO A GOOD LAND of brooks, pools, gushing springs, valleys, and hills; it is a land of wheat and barley, of grapevines, fig trees, pomegranates, olives, and honey; it is a land where food is plentiful, and nothing is lacking; it is a land where iron is as common as stone, and copper is abundant in the hills. (Deuteronomy 8:7–9).

I COME INTO EXCESSIVE WEALTH

> *For if you give, you will get! Your gift will return to you in full and overflowing measure, pressed down, shaken together to make room for more, and running over. Whatever measure you use to give—large or small—will be used to measure what is given back to you." (Luke 6:38) TLB.*

I will admonish you to find more scriptures to enable you to prophesy your way into prosperity.

End Note
  Dr Leroy Thompson Sr.
  Money Cometh: To the Body of Christ

CHAPTER FIVE

Field and Treasure

> *The Kingdom of Heaven is like A TREASURE that a man DISCOVERED IN A FIELD. In his EXCITEMENT, HE SOLD EVERYTHING HE OWNED TO GET ENOUGH MONEY to BUY THE FIELD—and GET THE TREASURE, TOO. (Matthew 13: 44) TLB.*

This chapter is based on the above scripture. Every field carries a unique treasure. It is easy to look at a field and walk away without realizing the potential in it. As men, we often look at things from a face value rather than seeing the things for what they are really worth. For this single reason, some have discarded their field(s) that would have brought them great gain. Your God-given field is your Promised Land.

After reading this piece of scripture, the theme "field and treasure" began to form in my heart. I knew that it did not have to stop there but I needed to dig deeper to reach the crux of the matter. It was then that I remembered a story my grandmother told me about the years that she used to travel from Akwapim to Accra to visit her daughters and also to buy items she needed for her trade. She would always see this large field before getting to Legon. This field was barely occupied. Those were the 70s and 80s and it never occurred to her to purchase a piece of that land.

Now as we speak, this large field has become a metropolis with some of the best estates in Ghana. She tells me she regrets not buying then. Now a piece of land in that area has so much appreciated in value that you require much more money to make a purchase.

Back to field and treasure. According to the Illustrated Dictionary of the Bible, a field is a plot of open ground that might be used for different purposes. The purpose could be for planting crops, raising livestock, hunting game, building a house or for a particular event.

Treasure, on the other hand, is an accumulated or store of wealth in the form of money, jewels or other valuables, according to the Free Online Dictionary. Just by definition alone, I believe there is a lot to learn. Your field is simply the place where your strength, abilities, potential and gifts are best harnessed. It is also the place where one finds fulfilment or joy in what he /she does best. You could be trained in a particular area but what you are best at might not have any relation with your training. The secret to finding your field is this—anything you do with joy, ease and are willing to die for if need be is your allotted field.

Your field might not be popular to the mainstream but do not be discouraged by the opinions of others. Therefore, do not vacate your field for any other thing. Not too long from now, your glory will appear to all.

Now let me come to treasures. However small they may look like, do not undervalue their worth. A treasure is a treasure no matter how it may look like its raw state. Gold, diamond and gems, in general, are never found on the shallow surface of the earth; rather, excavation is required to get them out. These elements may look like any other stone shrouded in dirt but the beauty is that once it is identified and worked on, wealth will be generated. So it is with all treasures.

In writing this chapter, I decided to look at what the commentaries of Matthew Henry, Pulpit and other writers have got to say about this scripture and here are the findings—"the setting here presupposes that someone has buried a treasure and later died. The current owner of the field is unaware of its existence. The finder, perhaps a farm labourer, is entitled to it, but is unable to conveniently extract it unless he buys the field. For a poor peasant, such a discovery of treasure represented the "ultimate dream."

"If a man had found a treasure in loose coins among the corn, it would certainly be his, if he bought the corn. If he had found it on the ground, or in the soil, it would equally certainly belong to him, if he could claim ownership of the soil, and even if the field were not his own, unless others could prove their right to it. The law went so far as to adjudge to the purchaser of fruits anything found among these fruits" (Edersheim, 'Life,' 1:595).

LESSONS TO BE LEARNT

- Discover your field. Do not rest until you identify your given field. Once you discover it, do everything possible to possess it. I have said over and again that we discover with the intention to settle down and once we are able to settle down, we place a demand on ourselves to advance in that area.

- Conceal that which is precious to you from others until it is right and appropriate for the time of its manifestation. The man in the parable hid the treasure when he found it, with the sole intention to come back for it. There are certain things that are for your eyes only. Like most motion pictures, what happens behind the scenes on most occasions are not captured for public consumption.

- The excitement/joy/thrill factor cannot be overemphasised. Excitement is the energy that drives your dreams to reality. Another word for excitement is enthusiasm. When enthusiasm is out of the way, tenacity is lost. Joy gives one the enduring power. The man in the parable kept his excitement alive that is why he was able to take a big risk of selling everything he had for this field or property. Excitement is what resonates and accelerate the manifestation of dreams
- Have a master plan. Planning is a vital ingredient for success. By the act of planning, you are able to measure your strength against your shortcomings. The man had a commodity (field, ground or property) before him to buy but knowing well he did not have enough money to purchase it, he had to come up with a plan to aid him in acquiring the field.

I believe he sat down to figure his way out. Questions like "what can I do on my part to get this money?" must have surely been on his mind. Normally, when we want to raise capital, we first think of "OPM"—Other People's Money. That is asking family and friends for their help. Watch this, for the man, neither OPM nor the bank was his option for raising capital.

On this particular occasion, he figured he had to sell all he had to enable him to buy the field. He took the risk, did a benefit analysis and finally realised that the benefits far outweighed the risk. This decision led him to buy the field.

- The art of selling and buying was deployed to enable him to get to the next level of his life. He sold what he had to buy a field that had equity and higher returns than anything he once owned. What do you have that you can sell?

- He was ready to get his hands dirty even after he had purchased the field. How do I know this? He was the only one who knew the location of the treasure in the field. The late Archbishop Benson Idahosa once said, *"the palms of a gold miner are rough but his bank account is smooth".* I agree with him.

  The decision to buy was not a pleasant experience; it is like the roughness of the palms of a gold miner. However, the benefit that awaited him superseded the initial pain and roughness he initially went through at the decision level.

- Could it be that the previous occupant was sitting on a pile of wealth unknowingly? It took another eye on the part of the farm worker to see the treasure in the field. It is expedient that you have another eye if you so desire to succeed in life and ministry.

- Discussion or talks behind closed doors are important in your venture to possess your field. I believe the man talked over with the original owner about his willingness to give an offer for the field.

Based on that, he was bold to put all his eggs in one basket. In other words all his money into buying the field. The principle here is that make sure you have your feet firmly on the field and treasure before you make an unconditional commitment.

- He was anticipating a change in his life. Within the period, he sealed the transaction to purchase the field. That fateful day, his position, status and reputation shifted from a farm worker to a landowner. Can you imagine that?

- He took the field as the business of his life. The activity on the field was going to define his livelihood. So then, the activity in the field would determine the flow of wealth in his life. My question to you is, how active in your field?

- Despise not small things. Small does not mean nothingness. For all you know, that small treasure found was an indication that the whole field was full of treasures. The daunting challenge for him would be whether he should go after the treasure in the field or keep to himself what he already had aforethought.

- The kingdom of God was likened to this man in the parable. When you see somebody or an organisation doing what exactly is in your heart, then such person or organisation becomes the model for imitation. We all build after 'likes'. Be rest assured that if the principles worked effectively for the kingdom of God and the man in the parable; then it will work for you too.

- The last principle is the God factor. God is the One who created the fields and the treasures, so you certainly need Him in gaining these possessions. *But we have this treasure in earthen vessels [men], THAT THE EXCELLENCY OF THE POWER MAY BE OF GOD, and not of us. (2 Corinthians 4:7 with the writer's addition).*

Your field may be sports, business, leadership, politics, education etc. Whatever it is, there is the need to begin to see ourselves in the light and life of this man in the picture, it is only then you shall begin to possess the field of your destiny.

End Notes

Herbert Lockyer, Sr. F.F Bruce, R.K. Harrison

Illustrated Dictionary Of The Bible

Matthew Henry Commentary

Pulpit Commentary

Parable of the Hidden Treasure

http://en.wikipedia.org/wiki/Parable_of_the_Hidden_Treasure

Matthew 13:44 "The Kingdom Of Heaven Is Like Treasure Hidden In A Field" http://biblehub.com/matthew/13-44.htm

Archbishop Benson Idahosa

Sermon

CHAPTER SIX

Aspire

> *Before this chapter rolls out, let us look up the word aspire in the dictionary. It reads—to desire with eagerness, to seek to attain something high or great. There is no great achievement on earth that has been accomplished without the element of aspiration.*

So then, when you see the rich and influential, aspire to be like them and in no way should you envy them. Those who envy the rich in their hearts have not got anywhere with it. The secrets of the rich are what you have to listen to and learn from; for in them lie the processes and frameworks that made them. There is nothing wrong in aspiring to be rich.

When we were growing up as children, we all aspired to be one thing or the other as adults. An aspiration is what kept the fire of those dreams glowing. Overtly, some gave up on their dreams because some challenges beyond their control knocked them off their feet. You were really doing fine until that challenge set in and since then you have not discovered yourself.

Now is the time to bounce back. Failure in one endeavour does not mean the end of the world. Pick yourself up and let that pains caused by the challenges energize you to aspire again. I said all this to let you hope again, aspire again and believe again that you can be rich regardless of the failures of the past.

> *And in the fourth watch of the night Jesus went unto them, walking on the sea. And when the disciples saw him walking on the sea, they were troubled, saying, It is a spirit; and they cried out for fear. But straightway Jesus spake unto them, saying, Be of good cheer; it is I; be not afraid. And Peter answered*

him and said, Lord, if it be thou, bid me come unto thee on the water. And he said, Come. And when Peter was come down out of the ship, he walked on the water, to go to Jesus. But when he saw the wind boisterous, he was afraid; and beginning to sink, he cried, saying, Lord, save me. And immediately Jesus stretched forth his hand, and caught him, and said unto him, O thou of little faith, wherefore didst thou doubt? (Matthew 14:25–31).

Before I come to this scripture, let me walk you through this story. My sister and I used to spend some of our weekends with our relatives on the University of Ghana Campus, precisely Little Legon. I loved those times I spent with my relatives. Those were great moments to me. What I also loved about those times was the fact that this environment was and still one of the finest places in Ghana where the crème de la crème of elites are raised.

Seeing these elites in this environment as a young boy, I aspired in my heart of heart to one day be a graduate. Today, I can boast of a degree and masters in the field of science and business respectively. I hope to aspire for more.

During those days with my cousins, I was introduced to the game of monopoly which was rare to find in most homes in Ghana in the 1980s. The lessons I learnt from playing those games still remain with me; they are somewhere in my consciousness. Directly and indirectly, I learnt the power and rules of money. Moreover, I have a dad who instilled in me the rudiments of what it takes to be rich.

There are about three things that drive me to aspire to be rich. Firstly, it is in seeing my own earthly father who God has blessed with riches.

Secondly, the early lessons I gained playing the game of monopoly. Finally, the immense wisdom I have found in the Bible.

Now back to the scriptures. Between the hours of three and six o'clock in the morning, I wonder what might be going through the mind of these disciples when they saw Jesus from a distance walking on the sea. A ghost they all thought but they were certainly wrong. It was a man (Jesus) who had the supernatural ability to walk on water.

For the very first time, Peter and the rest of the disciples saw Jesus walk on water. What a sight this might have been for them. They were stunned to behold such a mystery unfold before their very eyes. A new vista had opened for these men to step into the unknown. The thing is, it is only Peter who aspired to walk where the Master was walking: on water. Believe it or not, it was aspiration that drove Peter to venture into this new territory.

After hearing such an inspiring word *"be of good cheer"*, Peter could not help it but respond in this manner *"bid me to come"* on the water with you. It is time to step out of your comfort zone into something new.

For a moment, Peter forgot about the fear of losing his life in this phenomenal attempt to walk on water. In our human experience on earth, it is Peter who happens to be the second man to have walked on water. What a marvel it was for him to walk where no man had ever walked except Jesus. I believe that this particular experience will stay with Peter for the rest of his life.

When you see someone do what you have never done, ask them to introduce you to that world.

SET YOUR FACE

> *Because the Sovereign LORD helps me, I will not be disgraced. Therefore have I SET MY FACE LIKE A FLINT, and I know I will not be put to shame. He who vindicates me is near. (Isaiah 50:7,8a) NIV.*

There are those who think it is not worth aspiring to be rich, so they settle for anything. It is not a waste of time aspiring to be something that you are not now. Almost all the rich people you will come across will tell you that at a point in their life, they purposed to become something.

The day you set your face before God and creation to prosper at all cost, you will discover enormous help that is all around; for you to move into the territory of abundance. Help is going to come from God and people as well. Say aloud: help is on the way.

God is ever near to claim the right to your financial success. I personally love the expression *"I set my face like a flint"*. For those who do not know what a flint is; it is hard and unyielding fine-grained quartz which has the ability to produce a spark or fire when struck. In relating the word flint to this message, I can say it is required of you to develop an unyielding mindset and passion to come into your ordained place in prosperity. Disgrace and shame have been commanded to leave you for good in Jesus name. Say amen to that.

ELEVEN THINGS YOU HAVE TO ASPIRE TO IN LIFE

1. To Gain A Good Education

One of the ways to get out of poverty is to gain a good education. Those who have attained higher education normally tend to have middle-income status and with an extra effort on their part can break into the region of the wealthy.

2. To Own A Shop

Money attends to people who run a shop or a business. Some run their businesses from home while the giant retailers operate at the broadways. Having once been a shop assistant with Woolworths PLC, Wimbledon, I can boldly tell you that there is nothing like running a business on broadways. People come from every walk of life just to buy things to meet their needs.

3. Become A Giver or Philanthropist

> *Happy [Blessed, Fortunate, Enviable] is the man who CARES for the poor. The Lord will save him in times of trouble. The Lord will keep him alive and safe. And he will be happy [extremely favoured, powerful and mighty] upon the earth. You will not give him over to the desire of those who hate him. The Lord will give him strength on his bed of sickness. When he is sick, You [the Lord] will make him well again. (Psalm 41:1–3 additions made by the writer) NLV.*

There is a common default in life and it works perfectly well for anyone who knows how to work it; it is all about giving and continually giving. To church folks, it is called giving and the world chooses to call it philanthropic work.

As you aspire to become the person you want to be, life adds the virtue of caring for others as part of your status in life. I have found out that there are six things at the disposal of a man or woman who thinks about and ministers to need of others.

> Happy, blessed and enviable is the life of these givers. (Psalm 41:1a).
>
> Deliverance from troubles and even in trouble a way of escape awaits them (Psalm 41:1b).
>
> The Lord takes up the responsibility to keep these ones alive, safe and sound. (Psalm 41:2).
>
> Creation pays attention to these people. The earth counts it a privilege to have these people to walk and live it. Indeed the label of the "mighty in the land" is accorded to givers or philanthropists. I call them newsmakers. (Psalm 41:2)
>
> The will of their enemies will be frustrated. For in vain do their enemies plot against them. (Psalm 41:3).
>
> In sickness and out of sickness, the Lord administers strength to them. The easy way to cheat sickness is by giving. (Psalm 41:3).

4. To Own A Home

You must desire to become a rent-free person. You cannot go on serving other people month by month and expect to be rich. Buy a land, start the foundation and keep at it and with time you will roof and wall the house. Have a winning and workable plan if mortgage is your option. Do your best to shorten the time on this mortgage facility you have contracted or are about to contract.

5. To Own A Car

The days of having a car as a luxury is gone. Moving from here to there will require a means of transport. Waiting for a bus and a train is good but to have your own means of transport is great and it will save you time.

6. To Have An Investment Portfolio

Have a mind to invest a part of your salary and you will be amazed as to how much this yields over the years. Take a close look at where you are putting your eggs so that when the time is due for the hatching of chickens, you know how much will be coming into your account.

7. To Drink Well, Eat Well and Dress Well

Your life is of more value than anything in your possession. It will, therefore, be wise on your part to drink and eat well. Junk food has the capacity to make you unhealthy so watch it. It is also said that men address you based on how you are dressed. Dress like one who is going to the palace or better still like one from the palace. Prosperity must reflect on you.

8. To Have Good Relationships

> *Friends love through all kinds of weather, and families stick together in all kinds of trouble. (Proverbs 17:17) MSG.*

Life has different weathers; at one point it can be all gloomy and at another point, it can be all fair. No matter how tough you think you might be, you might face some difficult condition which will demand help from a friend or a family member. As you aspire to be rich, remember you cannot do it all alone. You will need counsel or direction from someone in your life to aid you to get to where you desire financially. Friends and family will make inputs to help you get into wealth circle if only you will open your doors.

9. To Be Planted In House of God

And he shall be LIKE A TREE PLANTED BY THE RIVERS OF WATER, that bringeth forth his FRUIT IN HIS SEASON; his leaf also shall not wither; and WHATSOEVER HE DOETH SHALL PROSPER. (Psalm 1:3)

THOSE that be planted in the HOUSE OF THE LORD shall flourish in the COURTS OF OUR GOD. (Psalm 92:13)

Be planted in the house of God. Join a Spirit-filled, Bible-believing church and connect with a community of believers. By so doing, rivers of water will enrich your life. Rivers of water mainly will come your way by the Word and Spirit encounters that take place in the house of God.

Those who are planted in the house of God are rooted in an uncommon soil; so they are bound to flourish. Season by season looks good for them, so how can they wither (dry or decline)? Withering is not part of the package. How does it feel to be a "Green House" and be ever increasing in the area of prosperity? Note, God has already decided in His courts to prosper you and it cannot be reversed. Having said that, never endeavour to leave His house when He prospers you.

10. To Be A Soul Winner

The fruit of the [uncompromisingly] righteous is a tree of life, and HE WHO IS WISE CAPTURES HUMAN LIVES [FOR GOD, AS A FISHER OF MEN—HE GATHERS AND RECEIVES THEM FOR ETERNITY]. (Proverbs 11:30) AMP.

The winning of souls is a prerogative for all Christians. Become a fisher of men today because if you do not, many are heading towards eternity without God. I believe you cannot stand it seeing loved ones, friends, neighbours and masses heading towards eternal damnation. It is, therefore, vital for us all to invest our time, energy, prayers and money to see as many saved as possible.

11. To Have Friendship With God.

"Now acquaint yourself with Him, and be at peace; THEREBY GOOD WILL COME TO YOU. Receive, please, instruction from His mouth, And lay up His words in your heart. If you return to the Almighty, you will be BUILT UP; You will remove iniquity far from your tents. Then you will LAY YOUR GOLD IN THE DUST, And the gold of Ophir among the stones of the brooks. YES, THE ALMIGHTY WILL BE YOUR GOLD AND YOUR PRECIOUS SILVER; For then you will have your delight in the Almighty, And lift up your face to God. You will make your prayer to Him, He will hear you, And you will pay your vows. YOU WILL ALSO DECLARE A THING, AND IT WILL BE ESTABLISHED FOR YOU; So light will shine on your ways. When they cast you down, and you say, 'EXALTATION WILL COME!' Then He will save the humble person. (Job 22:21–29) NKJV.

11. To Have Friendship With God.

I intentionally reserved the best for the last. Friendship with God cannot be downplayed if you aspire to make it in life. For me, the best place to be in life is to become a close friend of God. It is a place where you are at liberty to be yourself. An inexplicable peace becomes your portion through this wonderful union. To be at peace with yourself and with God is more than money. Just take a look at the benefits that come to you by this union:

- Good will come your way.
- Free advice from the Only Wise God.
- Reconciliation with God.
- Built up.
- Your tent becomes sin-free, therefore allowing God's glory to come in.
- God will lay gold as dust.
- God becomes your treasure.
- God becomes your delight.
- Get answers to your prayers.
- Shining or brilliance becomes part of your nature.
- Crown with exaltation.
- Salvation becomes your hallmark.

CHAPTER SEVEN

The Power Of Reserves

In our present world, you will hear things like a reserved seat, ticket, allotment, land, park, money, food, city etc. In my quest to know more, I was fascinated to find from the dictionary that the word reserve means: to keep in store for future or special use. It went on to say that in Great Britain, a reserve is the gold kept on hand by the Bank of England, whereas in the United States of America, it is the lawful money the National Bank holds on hand against deposits.

To the layman, it is the money at hand to meet or pay liabilities. We can conclude that a reserve can be in a form of paper notes, asset, liquid form or gold bars. A reserve(s), then, is vital to any nation's economy and an individual's financial status.

Currently, in the world of finance, the word reserve plays a big role in whether there will be a boom or a shortage of funds in world trade. I want you to know that the word reserve is not something new to this world we live in. In ancient times, a food reserve was what made Egypt a superpower. Let us take a quick look at the scriptures.

The abundance in the land will not be remembered, because the famine that follows it will be so severe. The reason the dream was given to Pharaoh in two forms is that the matter has been firmly decided by God, and God will do it soon. "And now let Pharaoh look for a discerning and wise man and put him in charge of the land of Egypt. Let Pharaoh appoint commissioners over the land to take a fifth of the harvest of Egypt during the seven years of abundance. They should collect all the food of these good years that are coming and store up the grain under the authority of Pharaoh, to be kept in the cities for food.

> *This food should be held in RESERVE for the country, to be used during the seven years of famine that will come upon Egypt, so that the country may not be ruined by the famine." The plan seemed good to Pharaoh and to all his officials...When the famine had spread over the whole country, Joseph opened all the storehouses and sold grain to the Egyptians, for the famine was severe throughout Egypt. And all the world came to Egypt to buy grain from Joseph, because the famine was severe everywhere. (Genesis 41: 33–37,56,57)*

It is this food reserve that made Egypt thrive in the face of drought. As a people, they were not perturbed because they had abundance in their reserves to see them through. In a moment just think about what would have happened to Egypt and the world if they had no food reserves. Starvation and death would have been everywhere.

Now, I would like us to take another perspective of reserves. Largely speaking, tapping natural resources beneath the earth crust has the potential to transform a nation. There is much more in the earth than what meets the eye. Oil, gold, diamond and other reserves have literally changed the financial landscapes of neighbourhoods and nations.

The thing here is that these reserves are beneath the earth (soil and water bodies) and it requires men and women with vision and drive to get it out. The moment these reserves are tapped, it blesses all directly or indirectly.

The principle here is that unlocking anything in your life will require energy and effort on your part.

Do you know that the Kingdom of Heaven places value on reserves? When you talk about extra, you are talking about reserves. Extra oil, extra money, extra food, extra room, extra space, extra times are all extremely important in the dynamics of any economy.

> *Then the kingdom of heaven shall be likened to ten virgins who took their lamps and went to meet the bridegroom. FIVE OF THEM WERE FOOLISH (thoughtless, without forethought) and FIVE WERE WISE (sensible, intelligent, and prudent). For when the foolish took their lamps, THEY DID NOT TAKE ANY [EXTRA] OIL WITH THEM; But the wise took flasks of oil along with them [also] with their lamps. (Matthew 25:1–4) AMP.*

The man or woman who knows how to handle reserves is wise and he or she has foresight for the future. Remember that all seasons are not the same. In the season of plenty, you must learn to create your own reserve; failing to do so comes with regret. An individual with reserves in his or her background need not go begging. Those who beg are thoughtless people. I did not say that; it is the Bible that said that.

> *Invest in truth and wisdom [reserves that come by your engagement with Heaven], discipline and good sense [reserves that come by your involvements in the Earth], and don't part with them. (Proverbs 23:23 with the writers addition) CEV.*

The scripture here is very direct about creating reserves for these four things - truth, wisdom, discipline and good sense. There are many things you have to part with on your way to the wealthy place but these four things are important companions on this journey. Invest heavily in creating this particular reserve without which you cannot succeed.

CHAPTER EIGHT

Acceptance of the Anointed Ones And The Prophets

Believe in the LORD your God, so shall ye be ESTABLISHED, believe his prophets, so shall ye PROSPER. (2 Chronicles 20:20).

And he said, verily I say unto you, No prophet is accepted in his own country. But I tell you of a truth, many widows were in Israel in the days of Elias, when the heaven was shut up three years and six months, when great famine was throughout all the land; but unto none of them was Elias sent save Sarepta, a city of Sidon, unto a woman that was a widow. (Luke 4:24–26).

The word "believe" in this scripture can be interchanged with the word acceptance. Your acceptance of God's prophet to you is certainly your gateway to prosperity. The entire nation of Israel was undergoing famine and during those days God sent a prophet by name Elijah to a woman who lived in the city of Sidon, outside the region of Israel.

This woman had limited resources to sustain herself and her child through those years. It was at that time that God sent Elijah to this woman for her to take care of him. Israel did not honour this great prophet; instead, he was a target of destruction for the King and his army. This widow in question honoured the anointing on Elijah; so amidst the great famine, she and her family enjoyed superabundance. This widow had an open heaven over her life and household and for that matter, she could not be moved or bothered with the hardship in the city. This woman was established in prosperity. What a way to live!

Jesus made a profound statement which is worth looking into—*"No prophet is accepted in his own country"*. Prophets are humans as any other body but there comes a time and a moment in their lives when the Spirit (glory, power, authority and grace) begins to move them in a particular way that overrules the natural order of things.

Since most people are used to how these prophets were naturally raised, it becomes very difficult to accept them when they are commissioned into ministry. Even Jesus—the greatest prophet above all prophets including Moses, Elijah, John the Baptist—remarked, *"I came unto my own but they received me not." (John 1:11)*.

For you to accept someone, you must first recognise the person. The recognition of these prophets does not take place so they are not accepted among their own people (country folks). On the other hand, there are those who have no knowledge of the upbringing of these prophets so they easily and readily receive them. The messages and instructions from these prophets certainly become beneficial to these people or group.

Get this truth: your acceptance of a prophet is also the acceptance of the One [God] who sent him. The reverse is also true—your rejection of a sent prophet to you is also a rejection of God. In this present generation where people have abused the office prophets, it will be expedient on your part to discern the right ones from the false ones.

Furthermore, a prophet's word can change a season. Elisha in his days prophesied, *"Listen to the message from the LORD! THE LORD SAYS,*

'ABOUT THIS TIME TOMORROW, THERE WILL BE PLENTY OF FOOD, AND IT WILL BE CHEAP AGAIN. A person will be able to buy a basket of fine flour or two baskets of barley for only one shekel in the marketplace by the city gates of Samaria.'" (2 Kings 7:1) ERV.

After this bold declaration, a fine measure of flour was sold for a shekel and two measures of barley for a shekel within the gate of Samaria. An advisor (economic analyst), on whose hand the King leaned, dishonoured and rejected the words of the prophet outright by saying if *"the LORD make windows in heaven, might this thing be?" (2 Kings 7:2)*. He questioned the integrity and efficacy of the given [inspired, prophetic, spoken, glory, rhema] word.

You know what later happened in this episode—the Advisor was crushed to death in the gates because of the human traffic after this outbreak of miracle. Indeed, this man saw the miracle but never tasted it. *There was one officer who always stayed close by the king to help him. THE KING SENT THIS OFFICER TO GUARD THE GATE, BUT THE PEOPLE KNOCKED HIM DOWN AND TRAMPLED HIM, AND HE DIED. So everything happened just as the man of God had said when the king came to Elisha's house. (2 Kings 7:17) ERV.*

This is a lesson for all and sundry—you better shut up when you are in doubt and when in doubt, doubt your doubts. Any time a season is about to change, God will send a messenger [angel, prophet and any of the five -hold ministry]. Therefore, a prophet's word can alter the course of a family, city, nation and nature.

In this case, Samaria was not an exception to this general rule. In a day, Samaria moved from great famine to superabundance. *Food prices dropped overnight and food became excessively cheap. God's word was manifested to the letter (paraphrased of 2 Kings 7:16) MSG.* The arrival of a prophet is an indication of a change in season.

CHAPTER NINE

Merchant Grace

Most preachers and teachers have highlighted giving and receiving as the central message of wealth creation for the people of God. As a result of these kinds of messages, there is a neglect of encouraging folks to become merchants.

Moreover, those who want to become merchants are often labelled as money lovers but this is a big lie. In my few years of being around, I have discovered the contrary-that Christian merchants are great supporters of the work of the Kingdom. They are often the first to give towards building church projects and also sending of missionaries.

The basic definition of a merchant is one who is involved in trade or commerce. A more complex definition is a person, company or an organization that is involved in:

- » Foreign trade
- » Wholesale trade
- » Retail trade

I remember listening to Pastor Andrew Adeleke, a senior pastor of House of Praise in London, commenting that when he moved to Peckham to start God's work among the people, he realised a common trait among the people and that was poverty.

So, he began asking the way forward to help his church members to be rich. The answer he got was to get the people to be skilled with their hands. He encouraged them in getting into masonry, floor tiling and plumbing works.

Now the rest is history, some of the very rich in the church today are these groups of men.

I will in no way downplay giving and receiving since I have witnessed its benefit and blessing in my life. All that I am asking is for us to retool our members with messages that will energize them to venture into the marketplace to reclaim for the kingdom of God.

I am the least surprised to hear the Master himself give a parable of the great pearl. Matthew 13:45–46 says it all *"Or, God's kingdom is like a JEWEL MERCHANT ON THE HUNT FOR EXCELLENT PEARLS. FINDING ONE THAT IS FLAWLESS, he immediately sells everything and buys it." (Matthew 13:45) MSG.*

There are lessons to be learnt from this parable. Here are some:

TIME

Hunting for excellent pearls requires time. Everything from the first step from the merchant's home to the place of finding this great or excellent pearl is time-related. Every finding in business requires time. Yes, every breakthrough in any field is a product of labour and time.

WISE USE OF MONEY

To ply the roads, cross the sea, board an aeroplane and make use of a restaurant and a hotel on this journey demands money. There is a tendency of not finding this excellent pearl and this could lead to the loss of money.

BUY CHEAP AND SELL WITH A MARGIN

Prosperity does not come overnight; rather, it is the gradual collection of goods and selling over time that brings in the wealth. Desist from buying cheap and putting exorbitant margins on it with the intention of making more profit. Small margins will bring in more customers and the more customers you have, the more profit it will create for you.

DEALS

Merchants are always on the lookout for good deals. Good deals are what bring money in business operations. Landing a good deal is like finding a gold mine. If you were to ask Donald Trump, Robert Kiyosaki, Richard Branson, Philip Green, Peter J. Daniels and other successful businessmen, they would all tell you that nothing works like a good deal.

The merchant in the parable was on the lookout for *"the deal of a lifetime"*. He was, in reality, going to sell all the pearls (jewellery) for the most valuable and precious pearl of all.

THE ART OF SEEKING

The art of seeking something precious and beautiful to have and to sell is the tenet by which merchants have lived through the ages. They always believe there is something out there for them and the people they carry at heart as customers. These merchants will go the length and breadth of the globe to find commodities or resources that will be needed in their homelands. Most of the time, they are seeking something out there.

BUSINESS SENSE

Every good and great merchant has a common trait and that is business sense. These merchants ride on the wings of business sense to build their various organisations. Business sense is what gives merchants a good feeling of buying trash to turn it into treasure. At a time of making decisions, business sense serves as a guide to the merchant to see beyond the corner.

Business sense is what makes merchants sense opportunities as well as threats in the marketplace. By this trait, men have been able to forecast and predict trends and even variations in relation to business projections.

With these same traits, merchants have been able to deepen their stack in the marketplace thereby making them a leading voice in their sector.

CAPACITY FOR STOREHOUSES

Merchants have storehouses or warehouses for the goods they sell. This house bridges the gap between the demand of the customer and the rate at which goods move on the shelves in the stores. One thing I must make clear is that every business has its own peculiar peak and lean seasons. Merchants, therefore, will buy goods when there is a boom, whether it is in its raw or manufactured state with the intent to store so that they can later sell with a margin on it.

Note that in the lean seasons especially, the merchant who has more of what the consumers are looking for will make a great profit.

ROUTES

According to Carroll Roberson in his book *"The Christ"*, the main caravan route that runs through Galilee was Via Maris which was north of Capernaum. Via Maris was a trade route for these merchants and the common story to hear on this route was the story of the day they would find the great pearl.

I will like to make a profound statement: *"your routes will determine your search; your search will determine your findings and your findings will bring you great joy"*. Every man who is in business will certainly tell you that he takes his route of doing business seriously.

You will find people who ply the routes of Africa, Asia, America, Europe and even the remote regions of the world just to find materials and businesses. Business relationships are established through routes. People find business partners and angel investors on these routes. Those who joke with their routes will soon be out of the marketplace—anyway they are going nowhere after all.

Your routes will determine the volume of business. By routes, you can raise your economies of scale. Your routes will create your golden connections and network with like-minded business individuals. Your routes determine receipts of business activities.

According to Forbes Africa Magazine, July 2013 edition, *"driving an economy without roads is never easy"*. In addition to this saying, I say running a business without routes is like a bundle of unending frustration of trying to use water from a borehole which is not connected to a running tap. The route is the gateway and essential part of the life of a business.

VARIETY

Merchants understand that men have different needs at different times; so, wisdom demands that variety be one of the hallmarks of the business. An ordinary pearl is cheap but an excellent pearl is certainly expensive.

When people, especially women, want to be outstanding in the crowd, they put on an expensive pearl (jewellery). Money is exchanging hands all the time; therefore, those who have a variety of goods stand a better chance of getting more money from buyers and consumers alike.

End Notes

   Cambridge Dictionary

   Carroll Roberson

   The Christ

   Forbes Africa Magazine

   July 2013 Edition

CHAPTER TEN

Releasing Your Nets For A Breakthrough

A great fisherman with great knowledge of the sea and a great sailboat who decides to sit at the shore with his nets by his side is in no way going to make a living. The potential of catching fishes is in view but the reality of catching a multitude of fishes just stays in the head because the fisherman has not made strides to go to the deep waters to release his nets.

*U*ntil the nets are released on the right side where the school of fishes is, the fisherman is bound on an endless journey of toiling.

And it came to pass that, as the people pressed upon Him to hear the Word of God, He stood by the Lake of Gennesaret and saw two boats standing by the lake, but the fishermen were gone out of them and were washing their nets. And He entered into one of the boats, which was Simon's, and asked him to put out a little from the land. And He sat down and taught the people from the boat. NOW WHEN HE WAS THROUGH SPEAKING, He said unto Simon, "Launch out into the deep, and let down your nets for a DRAFT." And Simon answering said unto Him, "Master, we have toiled all the night and have taken nothing. Nevertheless, at Thy word I will let down the net."And when they had done this, they enclosed a great multitude of fishes, and their net began to break. And they beckoned unto their PARTNERS, who were in the other boat, that they should come and help them. And THEY came and filled both the boats, so that they began to sink. (Luke 5:1–7)

Everyone yearns for a breakthrough but not everyone witnesses one. Before a breakthrough becomes a breakthrough, something must leave your hands or life to trigger it into existence. In this episode, Peter let go of his boat for

Jesus to use for a while. What do you have in your hands, will you let go of it today to create the needed breakthrough in your life?

Aside what I just said, I hear in my spirit *"there is a time for the washing and the mending of the nets but the right moment for the release of your nets is now. Not another time, because when the Teacher is done with his teachings it is the best time to cash in on what he said. There is a haul of fish is in your way if you will let down your nets for a breakthrough"*.

Before we begin to draw from the scriptures, I would like us to have a look at the word breakthrough. According to the Dictionary, the word breakthrough means to experience a sudden change of a situation, to make an important discovery, to make further rapid advances towards a purpose, to have a productive insight into a subject and finally to make a penetration in depth and strength into the enemy's defence.

With this in mind, permit me to highlight the major principles that initiate breakthroughs from the scriptures we just read.

Eight Principles For Financial Breakthroughs

1. Failure

You failed once and so what? That is not the end of the world. It is hard to believe that failure can be a platform for you to launch on to abundance. I do not know the business you are engaged in but let me bring it to your attention you are not the first person nor the last person to fail at an enterprise. When you fail at something, just laugh at the situation because there is another opportunity for you to try again.

2. You Need An Encourager / Inspirer

How forceful are RIGHT WORDS... (Job 6:25)NKJV

Jesus brings the right words at such low moments in Peter's career. We all need an encourager at one point or the other. When an encourager appears, it is a clear sign that the dawning of your breakthrough is near.

3. Make Use Of Your Kits / Expertise

As ordinary as you net [kit] may look in your eyes, it is the same kit that will pull in the abundance you so desire.

4. Step Into The Deep

Go a little further than where you have been before. Push a little more and better still make a bold and a giant leap into the *"Deep Waters of Doing Business"*.

5. You Are Surrounded By Miracles

A great multitude of fish is not a small amount of fish to have in your nets and must be the work of a miracle. Learn to make room for miracles in your financial matters. I personally believe that Peter and his partners left the lakeside excited because a miracle had taken place. Now, they could go home to their various families as real men.

6. You Need Helpers / Partners

On your way to your major breakthrough in your finances, you must learn to identify and to call for support from those who matter to your success. Just anybody will not do; you need people who understand where you've been and where you are going.

7. Work With Others Cheerfully

Peter and his team worked hand in hand to bring the fishes on board. Peter never stood aloof watching on; rather, the Bible said they worked cheerfully to fill both boats.

8. Crazy Instruction

Throw your net down. The best time for fishing is at night and not during the day. In spite of that, Peter was willing to obey this out-of-the-world instruction from Jesus. In short, it was the instruction that led to the breakthrough.

CHAPTER ELEVEN

Blessings Of The Patriarchs

> *This chapter was birthed as a result of the phrase used by St. Patrick of Ireland "I rise today in the prayers of the Patriarchs." Before we delve into the message, let's look at the word "Patriarch." A Patriarch is one who is a father or forerunner of a movement. So then, a word of blessing or prayer from such a person is of tremendous benefit to the one upon whom it is pronounced. Of a truth, "the lesser is blessed by the greater."*

It is the Lord that blessed Abram for it to be later known as the Blessing of Abraham. Here is the blessing: The Lord had said to Abram, "Go from your country, your people and your father's household to the land I will show you. "I will make you into a great nation, and I will bless you; I will make your name great, and you will be a blessing. I will bless those who bless you, and whoever curses you I will curse; and all peoples on earth will be blessed through you." (Genesis 12:1–3) NIV.

The making of a wealthy man or woman is by the Blessing. It is as easy as that. However, it is required of the receiver of this blessing to put this blessing to work. Idleness has never changed a life so do not try it even if you wear the blessing or the blessings wear you. By the blessing, Abraham went about raising cattle and digging wells.

Later this blessing would be transferred to Isaac and see what he does with it.

> *Isaac planted crops in that land and took in a huge harvest. God blessed him. The man got richer and richer by the day until he was very wealthy.*

He accumulated flocks and herds and many, many servants, so much so that the Philistines began to envy him. They got back at him by throwing dirt and debris into all the wells that his father's servants had dug back in the days of his father Abraham, clogging up all the wells. (Genesis 26:12–15) The Message.

After the impartation of the blessing, Isaac goes straight to work with it. One of the things he did was to re-dig the wells of his father that the Philistines had stopped up.

Isaac reopened the wells that had been dug in the time of his father Abraham, which the Philistines had stopped up after Abraham died, and he gave them the same names his father had given them. (Genesis 26:18) NIV.

If there is any lesson we can learn from one of earlier recipients of the blessing, Isaac, it is that:

» He recognised God as the source of the blessing.
» The blessing was of high value to him.
» He placed a premium on the family business.
» He put the principle of sowing and reaping to work.
» He did not change the names his father put on the wells. He had respect for the place and role he has played in his life and that of the family history.

What I am trying to bring to your attention in this chapter is that anytime you are in the presence of a father or a forerunner, cherish the moment, the words and the mantle on their lives. For one encounter with a Father figure can effect a good change in your life.

By now, you will be asking yourself: "the patriarchs have long passed unto glory, so how do I get this blessing from them?" The answer is simple: once you are born again [new creation in Jesus Christ] you qualify for this blessing.

> *That THE BLESSING OF ABRAHAM might come on the Gentiles THROUGH JESUS CHRIST; that we might receive the promise of the Spirit through faith. (Galatians 3:14)*

Now that you know you have the blessing of Abraham, let your spirit and mind become conscious of it. Boldly declare that the spirit of wealth is in your lineage and for that matter, you qualify to be wealthy. We all have seen how this blessing of Abraham has made the Jewish people stand significantly tall in the world's economy regardless of their small number.

What you are about to read next portrays the efficacy of the blessings of Abraham among the Jewish people. Mark Twain, one of the best writers in his generation, captured the impact of Jewish people on history. The following points are the full evidence:

- If the statistics are right, the Jews constitute but one percent of the human race. They look like a star lost in the blaze of the Milky Way. Hard to say, they ought not to be heard of but they are heard of, have always been heard of. They are prominent on the planet as any other people.

- As a people, their commercial importance is extravagantly out of proportion to the smallness of their number. The Jews' contributions to the world's list of great names in literature, science, art, music, finance, medicine, and abstruse learning are also away out of proportion to the weakness of their numbers.

- The basis of Jews success in business is rooted mainly in their honesty. In the history of commerce when it comes to a trader's trust in his fellow-trader, it was one of Christian trusting Jew and not Christian trusting Christian. This speaks volumes. Of a truth, a business cannot thrive where the parties to it cannot trust each other. No doubt the immense wholesale business houses of the Broadways are substantially in these hands.

- The Jew is not a disturber of the peace of any country. Even the enemies of the Jews will accept that. It is, therefore, not surprising that in crime statistics the presence of this people is conspicuously rare in all countries. In the police court's daily long roll of "assaults" and "drunk and disorderliness" these peoples' names seldom appear.

- The truth remains that the Jew is not a burden to the charitable organisations, neither of the state nor of the city the reason being that they are well knitted together. Indeed, the Jewish home is a home in the truest sense. It is a fact which no one will dispute. The members of this home show each other respect and when it comes to respect for the elderly it is not violated upon. This respect and strong affection among family members make them take care of the weak and incapacitated. They do this not in a poor and stingy way, but with a fine and large benevolence. The Jewish race is entitled to be called the most benevolent of all the races of men. When the weak and incapacitated is well enough and fully recovered, they work as they are supposed to.

- The charitable organisations of the Jews are supported by their own money and abundance; how about that? In finding this money and abundance to support their cause, they make no noise about it; it is done quietly - they do not nag, pester and harass other races for their contributions. The Jewish people express interest in the unfortunate so they generously give towards their upkeep which is a good trait for all to desire.

- Here goes Mark Twain again about the Jewish race—"He has made a marvellous fight in this world, in all the ages; and has done it with his hands tied behind him. He could be vain of himself, and be excused for it. The Egyptian, the Babylonian, and the Persian rose, filled the planet with sound and splendor, then faded to dream-stuff and passed away; the Greek and the Roman followed, and made a vast noise, and they are gone; other peoples have sprung up and held their torch high for a time, but it burned out, and they sit in twilight now, or have vanished. The Jew saw them all, beat them all, and is now what he always was, exhibiting no decadence, no infirmities of age, no weakening of his parts, no slowing of his energies, no dulling of his alert and aggressive mind. All things are mortal but the Jew; all other forces pass, but he remains. What is the secret of his immortality?"

- According to Professor Huston Smith, "Western civilization was born in the Middle East, and the Jews were at its crossroads. In the heyday of Rome, the Jews were close to the Empire's center. When power shifted eastward, the Jewish center was in Babylon; when it skipped to Spain, there again were the Jews. When in the Middle Ages the center of civilization moved into Central Europe, the Jews were waiting for it in Germany and Poland. The rise of the United States to the leading world power found Judaism focused there. And now, today, when the pendulum seems to be swinging back toward the Old World and the East rises to renewed importance, there again are the Jews in Israel" (Citation from Jewish Impact On The World)

- The fundamental social responsibility of our world is built on Jewish tenets which read, *"you shall love your neighbor as yourself: I am the LORD". (Leviticus 19:18b) NKJV.*

- According to the Talmud (a dossier of Jewish laws and traditions derived from the Old Testament), universal education was mandated for all Jewish people; it is only within the last 100 years this ideology is being incorporated into the fibre of entire world. Fast-forwarding this ideology into modern day, it is evident that everyone has unlimited potential for greatness and if given the opportunity will certainly become great.

- Today, in the Ivy League schools of U.S.A, about 23% of students are Jewish, even though Jews comprise just 2% of its population, says Hillel.

- Remarkably, Jews have received almost one-fifth of all Nobel prizes awarded since 1901. The contributions of the Jewish are really outstanding.

- The pursuit of the United Nations for world peace is encapsulated in the words of Prophet Isaiah a Jewish man: *"And they shall beat their swords into plowshares and their spears into pruning hooks: Nation shall not lift up sword against nation. Neither shall they learn war anymore." (Isaiah 2:4) NKJV.* The United Nations framework and work are entirely built on this scripture. The nations are now being charged by this framework to be committed to truth, justice, freedom, etc.

I brought all this up for you to see what is at your disposal. And if this Blessing of Abraham has made a remarkable difference in the lives of the Jewish people, then you are a candidate to express wealth and make a generational input.

I want to admonish you that regardless of your race, you qualify for the Blessing of Abraham through Jesus Christ. Coming into this blessing is by listening to God's voice and a blood covenant by Jesus Christ.

> *THEREFORE IF YE SHALL HEAR MY VOICE, and shall keep my covenant, ye shall be to me into a specialty of all peoples (ye shall be special to me out of all peoples), that is, a thing loved excellently; for all the earth is mine. (Exodus 19:5) WYC.*

End Notes

Modern History Sourcebook: Mark Twain "Concerning The Jews, Harper's Magazine, March 1898"
http://www.fordham.edu/halsall/mod/1898twain-jews.asp
Jewish Impact On The World | How Judaism Has Influenced Society
http://www.simpletoremember.com/articles/a/impactofthejews/
The 7 Wonders of Jewish History
http://www.simpletoremember.com/articles/a/7-wonders-of-jewish-history/

CHAPTER TWELVE

The Best Of The Land

> *There are quite a number of God's people who have reservations on the subject of prosperity. Some do not believe in it at all—for they feel and think it is a message of the world which has found its way into the Body of Christ. There are also those who believe in the message of prosperity and yet have gone overboard with it. They virtually merchandise that which they have received freely from the Lord. They forget this truth that freely they have received and freely must they give.*

*I*n either way, Jesus has a word for the former and the latter. To the former, Jesus says the poor you will always have with you. In essence, Jesus makes it clear for His followers that in no way should he be tagged with poverty. For Jesus came to make the poor rich toward God—even when it comes to money. Jesus even endorses the woman who poured perfume on him, for he says this woman had wrought a good work for pouring this expensive perfume on him.

For the latter, He will come into his temple with a whip to throw out the money changers. It is, therefore, important to present a balanced gospel of Christ on this subject of prosperity. It is in this light that I want show you how to enjoy prosperity without any trouble attached to it.

The land is before all and sundry; yet, the best in the land is gained by those who know how to access it. I am intrigued to find out from coast to coast and nation to nation that it is only a few who control the best of the land while the majority live to work for these few. Therefore, I can boldly say a few govern the majority all because "the best of the land is in their hands."

It is based on this that I am moved with a holy passion to teach the Body of Christ of how to come into the best of the land. There are a number of factors that can propel one to come into the best of the land.

Here are the factors:

- Willingness—the readiness or eagerness on your part to move into this realm of wealth.
- Obedience—you staying and compliance with God's instructions, leadings, direction, etc.

> *If you willingly obey me [GOD], the best crops in the land WILL BE YOURS. (Isaiah 1:19) CEV*

You must believe for the best, think about the best, ask for the best and accept the best. This should be the dogma that should govern our lives. None of us was designed to settle for the less.

Let us go further with this teaching by looking at the scriptures below:

> *Then their father Israel said to them, "If it must be so, then do this: Put some of the best products of the land in your PACKS and take them down to the man AS A GIFT—SOME BALSAM and SOME HONEY, AROMATIC GUM and RESIN, PISTACHIOS and ALMONDS. (Genesis 43:11) HCSB.*

Israel and his family were able to come into the best of the land of Egypt because they learnt to give their very best products in the form of gifts to the set man (Joseph) who was in charge over the food of Egypt and second-in-command to Pharaoh at that time.

Think about it, the best of balsam, honey, aromatic gum, resin, pistachios and almonds were given away in the midst of famine; this must be a crazy move and yet it was one of the keys that opened the doors for them in Egypt.

Now watch what this seed is about to trigger for Israel and his family. *So Joseph settled his father and his brothers in Egypt and GAVE THEM PROPERTY IN THE BEST PART OF THE LAND, the district of Rameses, as Pharaoh directed. JOSEPH ALSO PROVIDED HIS FATHER and HIS BROTHERS and ALL HIS FATHER'S HOUSEHOLD WITH FOOD, according to the number of their children. (Genesis 47:11,12) NIV.*

The district of Rameses was the most fertile land of Egypt and it was part of the royal city of Pharaoh; so, for Israel and his family to come into it effortlessly, it must be an act of God. Joseph gave them the best part of the land because Pharaoh willed it. This land would later be known as Goshen.

Remember, the principle still holds that what you sow is what you reap. In essence, Israel gave his best seed, Joseph, to Egypt who served these people well. In addition to Joseph, he also sowed his best gifts into the land; therefore, he deserves to reap the best of the land.

Taking this revelation further, whenever willingness and obedience meet, God unleashes the leadership capacity within us to enable us to choose the best of the land. Indeed, the best of the land will be ours if we let go the best that is in our hands for God and His work here on earth.

> *He chose the best of the land for himself because it is reserved for a LEADER (Deuteronomy 33:21a).*

CHAPTER THIRTEEN
Notable Giving

> *When we say something is notable, it simply implies that the thing is noteworthy, important and uncommon. There are groups of people and even individuals in the Bible whose giving were outstanding. Their giving caught the attention of Heaven. No doubt they are in the annals of God.*

Remember this saying of Napoleon Hill: "your action is your next move." Let your next move in giving count. If there is anything worth emulating, it should be their giving lifestyle. It is on this note that I will like us to draw lessons from them.

The Churches in Macedonia

Now I want to tell you what God in his grace has done for the churches in Macedonia. Though they have been going through much trouble and hard times, they have mixed their wonderful joy with their deep poverty, and the result has been an overflow of giving to others. THEY GAVE NOT ONLY WHAT THEY COULD AFFORD, BUT FAR MORE; and I can testify that they did it because they wanted to, and not because of nagging on my part. They begged us to take money so they could share in the joy of helping the Christians in Jerusalem. BEST OF ALL, they went beyond our highest hopes, for their first action was to dedicate themselves to the Lord and to us, for WHATEVER DIRECTIONS GOD MIGHT GIVE to them through us. They were so enthusiastic about it that we have urged Titus who encouraged your giving in the first place, to visit you and encourage you to complete your share in this ministry of giving. You people there are leaders in so many ways—you have so much faith, so many good preachers, so much learning, so much enthusiasm, so much love for us. Now I want you to be leaders also in spirit of cheerful giving. (2 Corinthians 8:1–7) TLB.

The churches in Macedonia had a notable grace for giving. This notable grace made them give and give beyond their means and measure. They gave even out their want (penury, lack).

According to the dictionary, the word notable means extraordinary, outstanding, remarkable, prominent, famous, important, noteworthy, or distinguished. So then, we can say that these churches in Macedonia gave far greater than other churches in other regions.

There is a great lesson for us all to learn from this scripture. Did these people experience deep poverty, trouble and hard times? Yes, they did. Did these people bury their heads in these times? No. Rather, they gave not only what they could afford but stepped into the realm of overflow with their giving. These people expressed much joy and enthusiasm for the fact that their giving was certainly going to be of help to the church in Jerusalem.

I think in today's church, we have settled in the arena of "what I can or we can afford" type of giving. So, whenever God calls us to step into the arena for complete dedication, giving over and above our means; we pull "a stop" placard before Him. Oh, Body of Christ let us not drift backwards; rather, let us advance in our giving. Whenever you come across notable giving, you will also take notice of good preachers in their company. My prayer is that we become leaders also in cheerful giving.

FOR IT PLEASED THOSE IN MACEDONIA AND ACHAIA TO MAKE A CERTAIN CONTRIBUTION FOR THE POOR AMONG THE SAINTS WHO ARE IN JERUSALEM. It pleased them indeed, and they are their debtors. For if the Gentiles have been partakers of their spiritual things, their duty is also to minister to them in material things. (Romans 15:26,27) NKJV.

Noah's Offering

And Noah built an altar to the Lord and took of every clean [four-footed] animal and of every clean fowl or bird and offered burnt offerings on the altar. WHEN THE LORD SMELLED THE PLEASING ODOR [A SCENT OF SATISFACTION TO HIS HEART], THE LORD SAID TO HIMSELF, I WILL NEVER AGAIN CURSE THE GROUND BECAUSE OF MAN, for the imagination (the strong desire) of man's heart is evil and wicked from his youth; neither will I ever again smite and destroy every living thing, as I have done. While the earth remains, seedtime and harvest, cold and heat, summer and winter, and day and night shall not cease. (Genesis 20:20–22) AMP

Noah touched God by his offering. It is this single offering that made God say no longer would he destroy every living thing like he had done before. Do you know an offering can stop a curse? Noah's offering stopped certain pending curses in the earth. Certainly, an offering can provoke an unending blessing. Anytime I see the rainbow in the sky, I remember Noah. Noah is dead but his offering still speaks.

King Solomon's Building Of The Temple

So Solomon built the temple and finished it. (1 Kings 6:14).

In 1929, the Illinois Society of Architects estimated the Temple built by King Solomon to be worth $87 billion. With 7% percent inflation rate per year factored in from 1929 to date, it should be more than $500 billion (cited Mike Murdock).

Enormous wealth really went to the construction of the Temple, Solomon built unto the Lord. In my research of the most expensive architectural buildings in the world, I came across:

- » Abraj Al Bait of Saudi Arabia which is worth US$15 billion. This is the most expensive building in the world today
- » Marina Bay Sands of Singapore worth US$5.5 billion. This is the second most expensive building in the world today
- » Resorts World Sentosa of Singapore, which is worth US$4.93 billion. This is the third most expensive building in the world today

None of these buildings is worth more in monetary value than the Temple Solomon built. This is a big surprise.

Cornelius A Man Of Giving

> *There was a certain man in Caesarea called Cornelius, a centurion of what was called the Italian Regiment, A DEVOUT MAN and ONE WHO FEARED GOD WITH ALL HIS HOUSEHOLD, WHO GAVE ALMS GENEROUSLY TO THE PEOPLE, AND PRAYED TO GOD ALWAYS. About the ninth hour of the day he saw clearly in a vision an angel of God coming in and saying to him, "Cornelius!"And when he observed him, he was afraid, and said, "What is it, lord?" So he said to him, "YOUR PRAYERS AND YOUR ALMS HAVE COME UP FOR A MEMORIAL BEFORE GOD." (ACTS 10:1–4) NKJV*

When we pray, it gets recorded in Heaven- so it is with our giving. Cornelius had a heart for people and more importantly for God. He was simply generous. Generosity can either be the little or big acts we do for people.

Anytime I think of generosity, I think of my dad. He opened our house to external family members to live with us. We all ate from the same pot. He gave to people near and far. He gave to friends and strangers.

When we talk about generosity, it is not doing things for people with the intention of they being able to do something for you in return. The true spirit of generosity says *"I want to be noticed in the eyes of God, not men"*.

I have been at both the giving and receiving sides of generosity. All I can say is that generosity has the power to touch the core of every human being. When generosity meets any man or woman in the path of life, it says can I help you.

This was how a gentile believer, Cornelius, was to the Jewish community. Regardless of his status in society as a prominent figure in the Italian Regiment, he exhibited a compassionate heart. What a way to live.

Let me encourage you in this when you do good and people take advantage of you, don't stop. Generosity has the power to schedule miracles for you. It was his generosity and prayer that triggered the angelic visitation. I believe a time is coming when God will send an angel to you.

I want to make an appeal to this generation: when we become a generous people, the world will erupt with the purest form of love. Give generosity the opportunity to manifest freely in you.

The Widow's Two Mites

> *Looking up, [Jesus] saw the rich people putting their gifts into the treasury. AND HE SAW ALSO A POOR WIDOW PUTTING IN TWO MITES (COPPER COINS). AND HE SAID, TRULY I SAY TO YOU, THIS POOR WIDOW HAS PUT IN MORE THAN ALL OF THEM; For they all gave out of their abundance (their surplus); BUT SHE HAS CONTRIBUTED OUT OF HER LACK AND HER WANT, PUTTING IN ALL THAT SHE HAD ON WHICH TO LIVE. (Luke 21:1–4) AMP.*

Most people normally give out of their abundance. There comes a time when the Lord will require you to give your all. In the widow's life, we are not told the Lord spoke to her to give her all. Out of her own enthusiasm, she gave what she was left with - two mites.

Naturally speaking, what she did does not sound right. From a spiritual perspective, she had put her faith on the line. To Jesus, she gave more and her best. This widow overlooked her natural conditions of lack and want. She stood against logic and human calculations and believed that God had the power to change her case.

I did find out from Psalm 112:5 of The Message Bible that those who place God's word above their present conditions can leapfrog in adversity. Take a close look at the scripture below:

> *Hallelujah! Blessed man, blessed woman, who fear GOD, Who cherish and relish his commandments, THEIR CHILDREN ROBUST ON THE EARTH, AND THE HOMES OF THE UPRIGHT—HOW BLESSED! THEIR HOUSES BRIM WITH WEALTH AND A GENEROSITY THAT NEVER RUNS DRY. SUNRISE BREAKS THROUGH THE DARKNESS FOR GOOD PEOPLE—God's grace and mercy*

> and justice! The good person is generous and lends lavishly; NO SHUFFLING OR STUMBLING AROUND FOR THIS ONE, BUT A STERLING AND SOLID AND LASTING REPUTATION. UNFAZED BY RUMOR AND GOSSIP, HEART READY, TRUSTING IN GOD, SPIRIT FIRM, UNPERTURBED, EVER BLESSED, RELAXED AMONG ENEMIES, They lavish gifts on the poor— A GENEROSITY THAT GOES ON, AND ON, AND ON. AN HONORED LIFE! A BEAUTIFUL LIFE! Someone wicked takes one look and rages, Blusters away but ends up speechless. There's nothing to the dreams of the wicked. Nothing.

I firmly believe that a seed given in faith to God can literally change the season of any man. I believe that these things happened for the widow:

- » The sun shone through the darkest hour of her life.
- » Her house started to brim with material abundance.
- » She was not perturbed with financial drought anymore.
- » She remained ever blessed.
- » God gave her another chance to live an honoured and a beautiful life.

It will not surprise me a little bit that God can do for you like He did for the widow. Add this promise to your faith collections – my children will be robust on the earth—as you give to God.

Cake For Elijah

> And she said, As the Lord your God lives, I have not a loaf baked but only a handful of meal in the jar and a little oil in the bottle. See, I am gathering two sticks, that I may go in and bake it for me and my son, that we may eat it—and die. ELIJAH SAID TO HER, FEAR NOT; GO AND DO AS YOU HAVE SAID.

BUT MAKE ME A LITTLE CAKE OF [IT] FIRST AND BRING IT TO ME, AND AFTERWARD PREPARE SOME FOR YOURSELF AND YOUR SON. For thus says the Lord, the God of Israel: The jar of meal shall not waste away or the bottle of oil fail until the day that the Lord sends rain on the earth. SHE DID AS ELIJAH SAID. AND SHE AND HE AND HER HOUSEHOLD ATE FOR MANY DAYS. THE JAR OF MEAL WAS NOT SPENT NOR DID THE BOTTLE OF OIL FAIL, ACCORDING TO THE WORD WHICH THE LORD SPOKE THROUGH ELIJAH. (1 Kings 17:12–16) AMP.

Cakes will be nothing to you when you can afford to buy groceries from any shop you so wish. The widow and Elijah did not have this kind of luxury especially in the middle of a heavy famine.

I recall that in 1983 my homeland Ghana experienced the worst drought in her history. I was young but I still can recollect the tough times we went through as a people. People had to queue for hours to buy bread. In those days, people found diverse ways and means of storing foodstuff for long periods. Yellow maize which then was reserved for the manufacturing of poultry feed became a hot commodity overnight. That was how bad it was. These are just a few examples. So, I tend to appreciate the value of the cake made by this widow. Tell me, what would be your reaction in this case? You and I would probably turn deaf ears to the words of Elijah.

Surprisingly enough, this woman responded in the affirmative and went ahead to bake the cake for Elijah. In the stretch of two and half years, this woman and her household enjoyed a *"miraculous provision"*. The jar of meal and bottle of oil never ran dry.

This story sounds farfetched but once the Holy Spirit has it recorded in the Bible; it is the truth. Always remember God can neither be boxed nor predicted. He does what pleases him. He is never accountable to mortal men but to Himself. Let this scripture below in the James Moffatt version of the Bible sink into your spirit.

ALL SCRIPTURE IS INSPIRED BY GOD AND PROFITABLE FOR TEACHING, FOR REPROOF, FOR AMENDMENT, AND FOR MORAL DISCIPLINE, TO MAKE THE MAN OF GOD PROFICIENT AND EQUIP HIM FOR GOOD WORK OF EVERY KIND. (2 Timothy 3:16,17).

Giving That Took Place At The Apostles' Feet

Neither was there any among them that lacked: FOR AS MANY AS WERE POSSESSORS OF LANDS OR HOUSES SOLD THEM, AND BROUGHT THE PRICES OF THE THINGS THAT WERE SOLD, AND LAID THEM DOWN AT THE APOSTLES' FEET: and distribution was made unto every man according as he had need. AND JOSES, WHO BY THE APOSTLES WAS SURNAMED BARNABAS, (WHICH IS, BEING INTERPRETED, THE SON OF CONSOLATION,) A LEVITE, AND OF THE COUNTRY OF CYPRUS, HAVING LAND, SOLD IT, AND BROUGHT THE MONEY, AND LAID IT AT THE APOSTLES' FEET. (Acts 4:34–37).

There is a TV program I love to watch whenever I am in the UK called "A Place in the Sun." Another TV program I love to watch when I am in the US is called "Property Brothers." These TV programs are about the real estate business and how people choose and make buys of properties. To me, it is fun and interesting to watch these programs.

I said all this to demonstrate the fact that people across the globe place premium on lands and houses. Tons of money goes around anually in the real estate business in the world. With this in mind, imagine some Bible characters selling their lands and property just to place it at the Apostles' feet. Do you think these people do not know what to do with their money? You are mistaken.

They were concerned about the pressing needs in the church. They wanted to be a conduit of blessing to others. When the distribution was done, their giving spoke volumes for them before God. They believed in the leadership of the day. The leadership was transparent with what the money was used for. The money was used to take care of the needy.

There was another key factor that drove these people to give. Here it is in Acts 4:34: *And with GREAT POWER GAVE THE APOSTLES WITNESS OF THE RESURRECTION OF THE LORD JESUS: and GREAT GRACE WAS UPON THEM ALL.* When people come to a place of giving beyond the normal, then these elements must be at work:

- » Great power
- » Uncommon witness of Jesus
- » Resurrections of all kind
- » Great grace

Kindly study them and allow God to bring you into it.

The People Brought Too Much In Moses' Days

> *Then Moses called Bezalel, Oholiab, and all the other skilled men who the LORD had given special skills to. And they came because they wanted to help with the work. Moses gave them everything the Israelites had brought as gifts, and they used these things to build the holy place. The people continued to bring gifts each morning. Finally, all the skilled workers left the work they were doing on the holy place, and they went to speak to Moses. They said, "THE PEOPLE HAVE BROUGHT TOO MUCH. We have more than we need to finish the work the LORD told us to do." Then Moses sent this message throughout the camp: "NO MAN OR WOMAN SHOULD MAKE ANYTHING ELSE AS A GIFT FOR THE HOLY PLACE." SO THE PEOPLE WERE FORCED TO STOP GIVING MORE. THE PEOPLE HAD BROUGHT MORE THAN ENOUGH THINGS TO FINISH THE WORK OF BUILDING GOD'S HOLY PLACE. (Exodus 36:2–7) ERV.*

Bezalel and Oholiab were the key leaders for the building of the Tabernacle. These men handled the gifts in the building of the Tabernacle. The Israelites from morning till night kept presenting gifts in order to finish the work. By the superfluous liberality of the people, these key leaders had to tell Moses they had more than enough to finish the work.

Moses had to send messages throughout the camp—*"no more offerings to be taken for the building of the Tabernacle"*. The people were literally restrained to give because they had provided more than necessary for the Tabernacle. This is really remarkable. I pray that the Lord bring us to a realm where we can "overgive" towards His work.

Before I end this chapter, the Holy Spirit brought to my notice that to those who give and want to be noticed by other men, it is not a notable giving no matter how big the offering may be. This kind of giving does not count and it is simply a flaunting of wealth.

The Holy Spirit brought this scripture to my remembrance in Matthew 6:1–4: *"BE CAREFUL! WHEN YOU DO SOMETHING GOOD, DON'T DO IT IN FRONT OF OTHERS SO THAT THEY WILL SEE YOU. If you do that, you will have no reward from your Father in heaven. "WHEN YOU GIVE TO THOSE WHO ARE POOR, DON'T ANNOUNCE THAT YOU ARE GIVING. Don't be like the hypocrites. When they are in the synagogues and on the streets, they blow trumpets before they give so that people will see them. They want everyone to praise them. The truth is, that's all the reward they will get. SO WHEN YOU GIVE TO THE POOR, DON'T LET ANYONE KNOW WHAT YOU ARE DOING. YOUR GIVING SHOULD BE DONE IN PRIVATE. YOUR FATHER CAN SEE WHAT IS DONE IN PRIVATE, AND HE WILL REWARD YOU. (ERV).*

End Notes

Mike Murdock

Secrets Of The Richest Man Who Ever Lived

Napoleon Hill

Images For Action Quote

Top 10 Most Expensive Buildings In The World 2015

http://themysteriousworld.com/10-most-expensive-buildings-in-the-world/

A Place in the Sun | Overseas Property for Sale | Buying ...
http://www.aplaceinthesun.com/

Property Brothers | HGTV
http://www.hgtv.com/shows/property-brothers

Pulpit Commentary
http://biblehub.com/exodus/36-1.htm

CHAPTER FOURTEEN

With or Without Money

Life is in seasons and these seasons frame our life experiences. So then, as you go through life, there will be seasons where you will be with and others where you will be without money. We all feel great when we have money to do the things we so desire. However, when we have less money or no money, we dislike those seasons.

Apostle Paul can attest to this truth; so in his writing he says, I KNOW HOW TO LIVE ON ALMOST NOTHING OR WITH EVERYTHING. I have LEARNED THE SECRET OF CONTENTMENT IN EVERY SITUATION, whether it be a full stomach or hunger, plenty or want; FOR I CAN DO EVERYTHING GOD ASKS ME TO WITH THE HELP OF CHRIST WHO GIVES ME STRENGTH AND POWER. (Philippians 4:12,13) TLB.

During those seasons where Apostle Paul had nothing (no money), he learnt how to tap into the help Christ offers. He doubtlessly received strength and power to be able to go through those challenging times. This truth is hardly talked about in prosperity circles but it is better we set the record straight.

I talk as a man who has been through the mail. Do you know that there was a moment in Jesus ministry where he had money but could not buy any provision for the crowd because they were far from town in a deserted place? Take a look at the scripture below:

When he heard it he went away by boat to A DESERTED PLACE, quite alone. Jesus feeds a tired and hungry crowd. Then the crowds heard of his departure and followed him out of the towns on foot. When Jesus emerged from his retreat he saw a vast crowd and was very deeply moved and cured the sick among them. AS EVENING FELL HIS DISCIPLES CAME TO HIM AND SAID,

"WE ARE RIGHT IN THE WILDS HERE AND IT IS VERY LATE. SEND AWAY THESE CROWDS NOW, SO THAT THEY CAN GO INTO THE VILLAGES AND BUY THEMSELVES FOOD." (Matthew 14:13–15) Phillips.

So what is the importance of money when it cannot buy anything? Think about that. Jesus our model for living was not over-dependent on money, rather he dug deep within Himself to produce a miracle of multiplying a lad's lunch to feed 5000men, besides women and children.

He told the crowd to sit down on the grass. *THEN HE TOOK THE FIVE LOAVES AND THE TWO FISHES IN HIS HANDS, AND, LOOKING UP TO HEAVEN, HE THANKED GOD, BROKE THE LOAVES AND PASSED THEM TO HIS DISCIPLES WHO HANDED THEM TO THE CROWD. Everybody ate and was satisfied. AFTERWARDS THEY COLLECTED TWELVE BASKETS FULL OF THE PIECES WHICH WERE LEFT OVER. THOSE WHO ATE NUMBERED ABOUT FIVE THOUSAND MEN, APART FROM THE WOMEN AND CHILDREN (Matthew 14:19–21). Phillips.*

This presupposes to me that money can fail but the power of God will not fail in the face of challenging situations. We can truly say with Apostle Paul and Jesus our Master that we can live with or without money.

MISCONCEPTIONS ABOUT MONEY

1. Money Is The Root Of All Evil

This expression is a wrong presentation of scripture. It should rather read *"the love of money is the root of all evil"*. If the first statement were to be true, then we better withdraw the use of money from our daily activities so we do not get contaminated with evil. This statement cannot be true because God says in Bible that we should not come before him empty-handed—in other words, we should come with money to bless His work. This kind of quote has made people shy away from making a million bucks when even genuine means of acquiring it are presented.

2. Money Is For A Favoured Few

This also cannot be true because no human came into the world with handbags of money. Therefore, anybody at all who knows about the dynamics of money can make and handle big money.

3. Money Is A Respecter Of Age, Gender, Certain Places And Education

This too does not hold water. Irrespective of age, one can make money. The ten (10) year old can come into wealth just like the forty (40) year old. In this age of technology, it is not surprising to see people make their first million bucks in their twenties and thirties.

Years ago, there was this notion that men are money-getters and women are the money spenders. However, as we speak today, women, as well as men, are generating tremendous wealth all over the world.

Money will cross any border; that is why it will visit the bank, the marketplace, schools and virtually everywhere as far as people are in sight. Money seems not to differentiate places; so it has visited and continues to visit the houses of those merrymaking and those mourning. You will find it in the slums as well as rich neighbourhoods. Any house at all can attract it. Money is liquid and that is why it is called currency (current money).

Indeed, money does not pay attention to education, though education can aid one to become more efficient to make more money. If money were to pay attention to education, then it will only be found with the learned. However, I have come across certain folks with no education at all and yet they command such wealth.

4. Stolen Wealth Is Sweet

There are certain people who will steal from their organisation and even nation to amass wealth for themselves and their families with the sheer intention to enjoy it. A note of caution: such wealth does not last.

5. Those Who Hoard Money Have More Of It

Some people like to hoard money because they believe that once it is kept safe in their vault, then they have more it. However, when money is put to work especially into good ventures, it generates more than when it is made to sit in a vault.

6. Let Use Money Anyhow For Tomorrow We Will Make More

Some people mismanage money today thinking that tomorrow will still present an opportunity to make more of it. A riotous living will take money from you.

THINGS YOU MUST PLACE ABOVE MONEY

There are things which I want to bring to your attention. These things you must place above money. When you do, your life will move towards utopia. I like what Eduardo Galeano said about utopia: *"Utopia lies at the horizon. When I draw nearer by two steps, it retreats two steps. If I proceed ten steps forward, it swiftly slips ten steps ahead. No matter how far I go, I can never reach it. What, then, is the purpose of utopia? It is to cause us to advance"*.

1. God

> *"YOU MUST NOT WORSHIP ANY OTHER GODS EXCEPT ME. "YOU MUST NOT MAKE ANY IDOLS. Don't make any statues or pictures of anything up in the sky OR OF ANYTHING ON THE EARTH or of anything down in the water. Don't worship or serve idols of any kind, because I, the LORD, am your God. I hate my people worshiping other gods…" (Exodus 20:1–5a) ERV.*

> *"SO YOU PEOPLE BE HABITUALLY AND CONSTANTLY SEEKING GOD'S REIGN (or: sovereign activity and influence; kingdom) and the fairness and equity from Him, as well as His justice and right wised behavior in the Way, which He has pointed out (covenant participation)—and all these things will be added to you! (Matthew 6:33) JMNT.*

> *SO, YOU SHOULD PUT THE KINGDOM OF GOD AND WHAT HE SAYS IS RIGHT FIRST [IN YOUR LIVES], then all these things [i.e., food, drink and clothing] will be provided for you.! (Matthew 6:33) AUV.*

> *BUT LET YOUR FIRST CARE BE FOR HIS KINGDOM AND HIS RIGHTEOUSNESS; and all these other things will be given to you in addition. (Matthew 6:33) BBE.*

When you look closely at the above scriptures, you will bear with me that these phrases speak volumes:

- » You must not worship any other gods except me.
- » You must not make any idols.
- » Or of anything on the earth
- » So you people be habitually and constantly seeking God's reign
- » Right first [in your lives]
- » But let your first care

God will not relegate his position for mammon (i.e. wealth, riches, possessions, money and gold). There are people in our world today who bestow greater allegiance to mammon than to God. I understand we have bills to pay and good lives to live but these needs not be done at the expense of your relationship with God. Whatever you pay allegiance to becomes your God. Money is to be used and not served.

2. A Good Name

A GOOD NAME IS MORE DESIRABLE THAN GREAT RICHES; to be esteemed is better than silver or gold. (Proverbs 7:1) NIV.

A STERLING REPUTATION IS BETTER THAN STRIKING IT RICH; a gracious spirit is better than money in the bank. (Proverbs 7:1) MSG.

A GOOD NAME IS BETTER THAN FINE PERFUME, and the day of death better than the day of birth. (Ecclesiastes 7:1) NIV.

A GOOD REPUTATION IS BETTER THAN A FAT BANK ACCOUNT. Your death date tells more than your birth date. (Ecclesiastes 7:1) MSG.

A good name cannot be bought in the shop; rather, it must be lived out. Never trade a good name for a few cedis, dollars, pounds and euros. At the back of your mind, say to yourself that if the vaults of this world are open to you, you will not trade in your good name.

3. Family, Friendship & People

> *Some of the Midianite traders approached. THE BROTHERS PULLED JOSEPH OUT OF THE WELL AND SOLD HIM FOR TWENTY PIECES OF SILVER TO THE ISHMAELITES. They took him to Egypt. (Genesis 37:28) NSB.*

Never trade your family, friendship and people in general for money. Joseph was sold by his brothers out of sheer hatred of his dreams. According to the Pulpit Commentary, Joseph was sold at the highest price for a lad being twenty shekels and thirty shekels for a matured slave.

His brothers' main aim was to get rid of him. They did not care about him. Their brother was to lose his freedom to slavery, while they went about enjoying the liberties of life. How cruel could they be? History has clearly shown that the root of slavery is embedded in the love of money. Slavery has been abolished; therefore, do not start another.

4. Character & Values

> *Ill-gotten treasures have no lasting value, but righteousness delivers from death. (Proverbs 10:2) NIV.*
>
> *Ill-gotten gain gets you nowhere; an honest life is immortal. (Proverbs 10:2) MSG.*

In today's world, people have many quick schemes for how to make money but they pay little attention to the development of their character and values. Certain people's values disappear when it comes to money issues.

5. Your Position & Your Office

> *And remember the angels who lost their authority to rule. They left their proper home [first estate]. So the Lord has kept them in darkness, bound with everlasting chains, to be judged on the great day. (Jude 1:6) ERV.*

Allow me to use angels to portray something that will be of benefit to you. Some angels lost their position and office all because they followed another creature instead of God.

In the political circles, there have been people who have lost their seat and influence because they chose to be corrupt. These politicians chose money over the national interest. That is how bad it can get when money becomes everything to a man or a woman.

6. Loyalty

> *Gehazi came in and stood before his master. Elisha said to Gehazi, "Where have you been Gehazi?" Gehazi answered, "I didn't go anywhere." Elisha said to him, "That is not true! My heart was with you when the man turned from his chariot to meet you. THIS IS NOT THE TIME TO TAKE MONEY, CLOTHES, OLIVES, GRAPES, SHEEP, CATTLE, OR MEN AND WOMEN SERVANTS. Now you and your children will catch Naaman's disease. You will have leprosy forever!" When Gehazi left Elisha, his skin was as white as snow! He was sick with leprosy. (2 Kings 5:25–27) ERV.*

> At last Jonathan said to David, "Go in peace, FOR WE HAVE SWORN LOYALTY TO EACH OTHER IN THE LORD'S NAME. The LORD is the witness of a bond between us and our children forever." Then David left, and Jonathan returned to the town. (1Samuel 20:42) NLT.

Some people's loyalty disappears in the presence of money. They prefer money to the years of loyalty they have put into the ministry, work and even nation. Gehazi preferred money to the ministry. From then on, he lost the mentorship of Elisha. He also became a leper—a stigma he would have to deal with. He became an outcast just like that and lost touch with his family and community. A man with an enviable future would have to settle for something he never desired in life.

Similarly, you will discover that in military circles, when one chooses to sell information for money above their vows, loyalty and nation security, from then on the Security apparatus or Intelligence will treat this person as a betrayer. He or she is not seen fit to be accorded the status of a citizen anymore.

Anytime I think of loyalty, David and Jonathan come to mind. It will be good for you to read the full story on them. Even after Jonathan's death, David went about looking for people in his friend's family to be a blessing too.

> DAVID ASKED, "IS THERE ANYONE STILL LEFT OF THE HOUSE OF SAUL TO WHOM I CAN SHOW KINDNESS FOR JONATHAN'S SAKE?" ... So King David had him brought from Lo Debar, from the house of Makir son of Ammiel. When Mephibosheth son of Jonathan, the son of Saul, came to David, he bowed down

to pay him honor. David said, "Mephibosheth!" "At your service," he replied. "Don't be afraid," David said to him, "for I will surely show you kindness for the sake of your father Jonathan. I WILL RESTORE TO YOU ALL THE LAND THAT BELONGED TO YOUR GRANDFATHER SAUL, AND YOU WILL ALWAYS EAT AT MY TABLE." (2Samuel 9:1,5–7) NIV.

David exemplified loyalty to an extent that he literally fetched for Mephibosheth. Moreover, Mephibosheth was restored to the wealth that belonged to his lineage by David's orders. David did all these acts of kindness for the sake of his love and loyalty to Jonathan.

7. Life

Beloved, I wish above all things that thou mayest prosper and be in health, even as thy soul prospereth. (3 John 2).

And a woman having an issue of blood [hemorrhage] twelve years, WHICH HAD SPENT ALL HER LIVING UPON PHYSICIANS, NEITHER COULD BE HEALED OF ANY, Came behind him, and touched the border of his garment: and immediately her issue of blood stanched. (Luke 8:43,44).

There have been instances where people have flown or have been flown over to other nations like the UK, USA, Switzerland South Africa etc because they needed the best medical attention. The life and health of these people come before money. What is the essence of having money when one's life is deteriorating?

The woman with the issue of blood did not stop trying to get the best medical attention possible. She spent a great sum of money trying to get her health back. The more she tried, the worse it got. Her blood volume kept decreasing because of the disease. During these searches for medical help, the weaker she became and the shorter her lifespan was getting. She eventually resorted to touching Jesus for help. Her life was instantly restored by the power of Jesus. This should tell you that life is more important than money.

8. Environment

> *THE EARTH AND ALL THAT'S UPON IT BELONG TO THE ETERNAL. The world is His, with every living creature on it. (Psalm 24:1) VOICE.*

Men's wellbeing is highly influenced by their physical environment. Men have become money-lovers so they care not depleting the ecosystem to make their bucks. I once watched a documentary on the 'galamsey mining' in Ghana and I was stunned by the effects of these illegal mining on the ecosystem. The water bodies were polluted and forest belts destroyed. These ecosystems would probably take a lifetime to be restored to their original state.

Most of these people who engage in such illegal mining do it because of the devastating effects of unemployment and poverty. Nevertheless, when we begin to look through the eyes of the future, we will discover a time when human communities cannot be supported by these ecosystems.

Today's gains against a troubled future will not help us. You and I are called to be keepers of our world. Let us, therefore, make our environments beautiful by our daily actions.

9. Attending Church & Spiritual Things

> *AND LET US CONSIDER HOW WE MAY SPUR ONE ANOTHER ON TOWARD LOVE AND GOOD DEEDS, NOT GIVING UP MEETING TOGETHER, as some are in the habit of doing, but encouraging one another—and all the more as you see the Day approaching. (Hebrews 10:24,25) NIV.*

Meeting with the purpose of seeking God is not a trivial matter us some people would have us believe. In the western world, most organizations pay a time and a half or double to their staff on weekends. It is no wonder some Christians prefer to work on weekends in order to make more money.

I will not shift blame on anyone but honestly, we have to encourage ourselves not to neglect the house of God; especially as we see the Day getting near. Always choose spiritual things over money. It sounds foolish to the natural mind but makes great sense to the spiritual minded.

10. The Future

> *SHE PLAYED FAST AND LOOSE WITH LIFE, SHE NEVER CONSIDERED TOMORROW, and NOW SHE'S CRASHED ROYALLY, WITH NO ONE TO HOLD HER HAND: "Look at my pain, O GOD! And how the enemy cruelly struts." (Lamentations 1:9) MSG.*

Money should not be placed before one's future. Our leaders (be it kings, chiefs, elders, fathers & mothers) cheaply give our stool lands out for few cedis and cars, all in the name of money. As a result of this act of theirs, the future generation would become servants in their own nation. This is typical of leaders in Ghana and other parts of Africa.

The love for money by leaders in Africa makes the sons of the land suffer and suffering they never asked for are rolled out to them.

The leaders never considered tomorrow so they chose money over the future of their people. When national properties are sold to foreigners and the indigenous live at the mercy of these foreigners, it is really heartbreaking. There is more wisdom in leasing lands and properties than selling out entirely to foreigners.

Having said that, you must personally come to a place where you make a firm decision not to sell what you have cheaply to others. Be a good leader in your own circles. Remember these Ghanaian proverbs:

"An army of sheep led by a lion can defeat an army of lions led by a sheep."
"A healthy person who begs for food is an insult to a generous farmer."

I call on all to begin to reconsider our future.

End Note

The Best: 72+ African Wise Proverbs And Inspiring Quotes
http://afritorial.com/the-best-72-african-wise-proverbs/

CHAPTER FIFTEEN

COVENANT BROKERS

The first time I would hear the phrase "covenant broker" was when I started to put this book together. I was fascinated by this terminology like you are now. Before we dig deep, we are going to look at the words "covenant" and "broker" separately.

The word "covenant" is an agreement, contract or treaty that exists between two personalities. Among these personalities, one should be a Deity and this Deity should be greater in every sense of the word. God is in this class. Every covenant involves blood shedding or without that, it is no covenant at all. As believers, we understand Jesus is the Lamb who shed his own blood to establish this covenant between God and us.

Who then is a broker? A broker is an advisor, dealer, negotiator and agent who runs the enterprise of an institution. In this book, our focus would be the Kingdom of God solely. Therefore, a covenant broker by definition is a kingdom agent with a heavenly treaty to finance the work of God here on earth.

Master, which is the great commandment in the law? Jesus said unto him, Thou shalt LOVE THE LORD thy God with all thy heart, and with all thy soul, and with all thy mind. This is the first and great commandment. And the second is like unto it, Thou shalt LOVE THY NEIGHBOUR AS THYSELF. (Matthew 22:36–39).

The fundamental work for a covenant broker is to love God and his neighbour. The proof of this love is in giving. There are things to which covenant brokers will give their attention solely to demonstrate this love. The list is as follows:

TITHE AND OFFERING

For I am the Lord, I change not; therefore ye sons of Jacob are not consumed... Will a man rob God? Yet ye have robbed me. But ye say, Wherein have we robbed thee? IN TITHES AND OFFERINGS. (Malachi 3:6,8).

Those who love God will not rob Him in financial matters but rather push His agenda on the earth. Why are tithe and the offerings important to God?

- The tithe represents the first and best part of your life and efforts. The tithe is the first tenth of all your earnings.
- So that the men of God will be well taken care of.
- To reach out to the needy in society.
- A man or woman full of love will go over and above what is required of him or her. To give as in amount in regard to the offering other than a tithe is your own decision.

PRAISE

Let the peoples praise You [turn away from their idols] and give thanks to You, O God; LET ALL THE PEOPLES PRAISE AND GIVE THANKS TO YOU! THE EARTH HAS YIELDED ITS HARVEST [IN EVIDENCE OF GOD'S APPROVAL]; GOD, EVEN OUR OWN GOD, WILL BLESS US. God will bless us, and all the ends of the earth shall reverently fear Him. (Psalm 147:5–7) AMP.

Covenant brokers know how to release praise in the earth. Praise is playing the strings of God's heart. Praise is about touching and elevating God. This becomes your first nature and habit. As you praise, your harvest begins to look for you.

Those who know how to praise God always have something to thank God for. No more complaining and worries in your world, because praise will produce what you are looking for. Do you know when your harvest kicks in, laughter springs forth? This will be your portion.

Anytime covenant brokers turn on their praise, they commit God to display his power. It is this power that secures what should rightfully come to us. Covenant brokers are well known in the courtyards of God. The verse below says it all.

> *THE LORD MADE A PROMISE AND GUARANTEED IT BY HIS OWN POWER. And HE WILL USE THAT POWER TO KEEP HIS PROMISE. The Lord said, "I PROMISE THAT I WILL NEVER AGAIN GIVE YOUR FOOD TO YOUR ENEMIES. I PROMISE THAT THEY WILL NEVER AGAIN TAKE THE WINE YOU MAKE. WHOEVER GATHERS THE FOOD WILL EAT IT AND PRAISE THE LORD. WHOEVER GATHERS THE GRAPE WILL DRINK THE WINE IN THE COURTYARDS OF MY TEMPLE."(Isaiah 62:8,9) ERV.*

GOOD HARVESTERS

Covenant brokers know that for them to indeed advance the Kingdom of God here on earth, they need to become good harvesters. The thing about good harvesters is that they depend on God for the flow of rains and fruits on their grounds.

I WILL GIVE YOU REGULAR RAINS, AND THE LAND WILL YIELD BUMPER CROPS, and THE TREES WILL BE LOADED WITH FRUIT LONG AFTER THE NORMAL TIME! And grapes will still be ripening when sowing time comes again. You shall eat your fill, and live safely in the land. (Leviticus 26:5) TLB.

"If you live by my decrees and obediently keep my commandments, I will send the rains in their seasons, the ground will yield its crops and the trees of the field their fruit. YOU WILL THRESH UNTIL THE GRAPE HARVEST AND THE GRAPE HARVEST WILL CONTINUE UNTIL PLANTING TIME; YOU'LL HAVE MORE THAN ENOUGH TO EAT AND WILL LIVE SAFE AND SECURE IN YOUR LAND. (Leviticus 26:5) MSG.

Long after the normal time, they still have fruits. Such an amazing thing to behold! Their grounds overflow with a bumper harvest so they can afford to be a blessing to others. There is always a continuous flow of harvest for covenant brokers. It is God who sees to it that it goes well with them. Decide to become a covenant broker today and see how your life would turn out to be.

CHAPTER SIXTEEN

Breaking The Cycles Of Poverty

> *How can I talk about getting wealth when I do not deal with breaking or destroying the cycles of poverty? Quite a great number of people have been imprisoned by this negative cycle. They work hard but have nothing to show for it. These two scriptures below say it all:*

> Because you DIDN'T SERVE GOD, your God, OUT OF THE JOY AND GOODNESS OF YOUR HEART in the great abundance, you'll have to serve your enemies whom God will send against you. LIFE WILL BE FAMINE and DROUGHT, RAGS and WRETCHEDNESS; then he'll put an IRON YOKE ON YOUR NECK until he's destroyed you. (Deuteronomy 28:47–48) MSG.

> *Shortly after that, God said more and Haggai spoke it: "HOW IS IT THAT IT'S THE 'RIGHT TIME' FOR YOU TO LIVE IN YOUR FINE NEW HOMES WHILE THE HOME, GOD'S TEMPLE, IS IN RUINS?" And then a little later, God-of-the-Angel-Armies spoke out again: "Take a good, hard look at your life. Think it over. You have spent a lot of money, but you haven't much to show for it. You keep filling your plates, but you never get filled up. You keep drinking and drinking and drinking, but you're always thirsty. You put on layer after layer of clothes, but you can't get warm. And the people who work for you, what are they getting out of it? Not much—a leaky, rusted-out bucket, that's what. (Haggai 1:3–6) MSG*

The reason why there is this repeated cycle of poverty in people's lives is mainly that they are not serving God wholeheartedly and they are withholding part of their substance (time, energy, money and best of resources) from God. When we learn to serve God with gladness of heart and with the abundance of everything we have, we will be shocked to see the level of wealth we will command.

Prophet Haggai also brings a new topic for discussion, which happens to be one of the factors for people having holes in their bags. These groups of people say "this is not the time to build God's house." The amazing thing is this, these same people will go about buying things, from clothing to cars and what have you. However, they have little regard for the work that takes place in God's house.

A life filled with famine, drought, rags, wretchedness and having an iron yoke around one's neck is not what we have been called to inherit. A life of service will cause little to give way for much. Moreover, when we eat and drink, we will be satisfied. When we dress we will keep warm and in no way will not be prone to diseases.

Finally, those who do not tithe and give will certainly find themselves in the cycle of poverty. I have had the opportunity to speak with people who are struggling with their finances and yet when you recommend to them "the principle of tithe, seedtime and harvests (giving and receiving)", they will tell they do not believe in it and it does not work.

For your information, what you do not believe in does not work for you and the fact that you have not put this principle to work does not mean it does not work. For many years, I have seen this principle work wonders in my life.

ARE YOU SURVIVING OR LIVING?

> *All the commandments which I command thee this day shall ye OBSERVE TO DO, that ye MAY LIVE, and MULTIPLY, and go in and possess the land which the Lord sware unto your fathers. (Deuteronomy 8:1).*

Many in the Body of Christ find themselves in the survival mode when they really should be living the abundant life. Barely getting by is the signpost for the man or woman stuck in the survival mode. Living from one pay cheque to the other is also another sign of survival mode. Survival mode will not get you over the cycle of poverty.

A revelation of 'Get Wealth' is what will put us into a world of abundance and overflow. Anywhere, any place, any man to whom revelation goes to, multiplication will be obliged to find its way there. A man with revelation is not concerned about getting by but rather he or she is waiting for a command to be a blessing to others. When you find yourself in a living mode, helping others becomes your chief delight.

Those in the living mode are always looking forward to making positive contributions to humanity. Those in the living mode are thinking of building schools, hospitals, roads, resource centres, and sustainable relief programs for the less privileged in society.

The question that comes to mind immediately is "how do I get out of the survival mode to living mode (abundant life)?" The answer is simple—observe to do. This three-word phrase can revolutionize your financial life if only you will heed to it. To me, this is one of the powerful keys in the Bible and in the universe.

Decide to observe the ways and life of the rich people in Bible as well as the rich in your days and make a resolution to put to practise what these people did and are doing; you will be amazed to the change you will see in your finances. Let's observe Isaac for example.

> *And there was a FAMINE in the land, BESIDE THE FIRST FAMINE that was in the days of Abraham. And Isaac went unto Abimelech king of the Philistines unto Gerar. (Genesis 26:1).*

Isaac was at the lowest point in his finances around this time and instead of having self-pity for himself, he took a step that naturally comes to all of us—he moved into the city of Gerar to sojourn there.

Then in the verse 2b and 3 of Genesis 26, according to the Living Bible, Jehovah Jireh appeared to him and gives him word *"Don't go to Egypt". DO AS I SAY AND STAY HERE IN THE LAND. If you do, I will be with you and bless you, and I give all this land to you and your descendants, just as I promised Abraham your father.*

God knew perfectly well that Isaac was about to make another move and this move was towards Egypt. I know there is some sense to move from place to place when things are not working, just to find the place that will accommodate and bring the best out of us.

What we need to do in such moments is to ask God (the Maker and Creator of our lives) to help us locate the best place (niche) for our gifts and potential.

You know what, it was God who told Isaac to stay because that was the place for his manifestation. The Bible goes further to say Isaac did something that was absurd to do in the middle of a famine. He sowed his precious seeds.

> *Then Isaac SOWED IN THAT LAND, and RECEIVED IN THE SAME YEAR AN HUNDREDFOLD: and THE LORD BLESSED HIM. (Genesis 26:12).*

So then for you to get to the pinnacles of prosperity, you must:
- Recognise the voice of God.
- Recognise your place.
- Recognise your seed.
- Sow.
- Expect a harvest.
- Then restart the whole cycle of sowing and reaping.

I would like to, furthermore, bring to your notice how the cycles of poverty have been destroyed by God in history. I confidently believe you can come out of these negative financial cycles you find yourself in.

JUDGEMENT FOR THE RELEASE OF WEALTH

> *As the sun was setting, Abram fell into a deep sleep, and a thick and dreadful darkness came over him. Then the LORD said to him, "KNOW FOR CERTAIN THAT FOR FOUR HUNDRED YEARS YOUR DESCENDANTS WILL BE STRANGERS IN A COUNTRY NOT THEIR OWN AND THAT THEY WILL BE ENSLAVED AND MISTREATED THERE. But I will punish the nation they serve as slaves, and AFTERWARD THEY WILL COME OUT WITH GREAT POSSESSIONS. (Genesis 15:12–14) NIV.*

Four hundred (400) years before a generation would exist, God prepared and informed the founding father of that nation that his descendants would certainly enter into a place (land) where:

- They could stay and work in the land as strangers. I presume that normally strangers are nomads; therefore, they dwell in tents.
- The land in which they dwell is not theirs and therefore will never be theirs.
- The descendants of Abram would serve others and have the people they serve as lords over them. I am wondering who Abram might have felt for the coming generations in his lineage.
- On the supposed day of their departure from that land, they will be compensated by amassing the wealth of that nation.

Note this in your spirit, all it takes to come out is a day. Your day of freedom is here. Never again will you return to this path of poverty.

MEGA RESTORATION

And I will RESTORE TO YOU the years that the locust hath eaten, the cankerworm, and the caterpillar, and the palmerworm, my great army which I sent among you. (Joel 2:25).

But this is A PEOPLE ROBBED and PLUNDERED, they are ALL OF THEM TRAPPED IN HOLES AND HIDDEN IN PRISONS; they have BECOME A PREY WITH NONE TO RESCUE, a spoil with none to say, "RESTORE!" (Isaiah 42:22) RSV.

No one in his right frame of mind wants to be robbed or to be plundered of his/her wealth and resources. However, the scripture says many have fallen predicament to this evil tool. As if this is not enough, these people have been trapped in financial prison houses and holes that they have lost all hopes to experience freedom one day.

A new day has dawned for all because Jesus the Deliverer, Rescuer, Repairer is committed to us to restore us on every side. The buzz word in the Heavenly host now is "Restoration for God's People."

Whom heaven must receive [and retain] until THE TIME FOR THE COMPLETE RESTORATION OF ALL THAT GOD SPOKE by the mouth of all His holy prophets for ages past [from the most ancient time in the memory of man]. (Acts 3:21) AMP.

God spoke your prosperity into being long before you got here on earth. This is the time for getting back everything the enemy stole from you. Restoration is also coming for your health, fortunes and all things that pertain to life and godliness.

It was God [personally present] in Christ, reconciling and restoring the world to favor with Himself, not counting up and holding against [men] their trespasses [but cancelling them], and committing to us THE MESSAGE OF RECONCILIATION (OF THE RESTORATION TO FAVOR). (2 Corinthians 5:19) AMP.

The power of restoration can create a continuous flow of favour with God and men. It is said that one day of favour is worth more than a lifetime of struggles. No more struggles but financial victories for you in Jesus name!

CHAPTER SEVENTEEN
The Legacy

Your history is your legacy. Throughout history, there is documented evidence of God reaching out to men in the area of giving. The list is really a tall order. God gave and still gives the following to men for free:

- Life (Breath)
- Spirit, Soul and Body
- Rain
- Sunshine
- Glory
- Honour
- Earth
- Sea
- Provision
- Unlimited grace and mercy
- Joy and happiness
- Love
- Laughter
- Forgiveness
- Friendship
- Sleep
- Seed
- Time
- Garden of Eden
- Ministry of Angels
- Holy Spirit
- His Son (Jesus)
- His Fatherhood

The list is unending. God always has his hands open to his creation. I want you to take your time to read and reflect on the scriptures below:

> *You open your hand and satisfy the desires of every living thing. (Psalms145:16) NIV.*
>
> *Generous to a fault, you lavish your favor on all creatures. (Psalms145:16) MSG.*
>
> *You constantly satisfy the hunger and thirst of every living thing. (Psalms145:16) TLB.*

It then behoves us as men to imitate our Creator. When you read the Bible, you will come across men who made huge contributions to the work of the Kingdom of God.

PEOPLE IN THE OLD TESTAMENT

Abel

Abel propagated the first fruit principle in his days. God has respect for people who understand and adhere to holy principles. Any time we practise the first fruit principle, whether in the giving of our time or money, it reminds God of Abel's legacy.

> *Abel also brought of THE FIRSTBORN OF HIS FLOCK and of their fat. And the LORD RESPECTED Abel and his offering. (Genesis 4:4).*

Noah

There is something that stays the hands of God from judging the Earth like Noah's days. What could be this one thing that is able to stop the Most Powerful God in His track? Noah's legacy—the burnt offerings he offered to God when he came out of the Ark with his family

> *Then Noah built an altar to the Lord, and took of every clean animal and of every clean bird, and offered BURNT OFFERINGS ON THE ALTAR. And the Lord smelled a SOOTHING AROMA. Then the Lord said in His heart, "I will never again curse the ground for man's sake, although the imagination of man's heart is evil from his youth; nor will I again destroy every living thing as I have done. (Genesis 8:20,21) NKJV.*

Watch what takes place after this sacrifice or giving. God decides to share an important revelation with Noah, which today is still one of the leading scriptures when it comes to prosperity and other subjects.

"While the earth remains, Seedtime and harvest, Cold and heat, Winter and summer, And day and night shall not cease." (Genesis 8:22) NKJV.

Abraham

Now it came to pass after these things that God tested Abraham, and said to him, "Abraham!" And he said, "Here I am." Then He said, "Take now your son, YOUR ONLY SON ISAAC, whom you love, and go to the land of Moriah, and offer him there as a burnt offering on one of the mountains of which I shall tell you."... Then they came to the place of which God had told him. And Abraham built an altar there and placed the wood in order; and he bound Isaac his son and laid him on the altar, upon the wood. And Abraham stretched out his hand and took the knife to slay his son. But the Angel of the Lord called to him from heaven and said, "Abraham, Abraham!" So he said, "Here I am." And He said, "Do not lay your hand on the lad, or do anything to him; FOR NOW I KNOW THAT YOU FEAR GOD, since you have not withheld your son, your only son, from Me." (Genesis 22:1,2,9–12) NKJV.

For Abraham to give his only son Isaac as an offering on the Mount of Moriah, it speaks volumes of his love for God. It was at this highest point of giving that God saw another side of Abraham in his walk with Him.

David

It was from the lips of this great King that we would hear in scriptures "I would not give anything that would not cost me." David had a spirit of giving that even his progeny would catch. This man is known to have prepared materials for the building of the Temple even when God told him his son Solomon would be the one to build it.

> Then the king said to Araunah, "No, but I will surely buy it from you for a price; nor will I offer burnt offerings to the Lord my God with that which COSTS ME NOTHING." So David bought the threshing floor and the oxen for fifty shekels of silver. (2 Samuel 24:24) NKJV.

Solomon

> And Solomon went up there to the bronze altar before the Lord, which was at the tabernacle of meeting, and offered a thousand burnt offerings on it. (2 Chronicles 1:6) NKJV.

Solomon was extravagant in his giving. In the tabernacle, he chose to give God a thousand burnt offering. He counted from one to a hundred, from a hundred to five hundred and could have stopped but went on to a thousand. Indeed, this man knew the power in sacrificing to God.

PEOPLE IN THE NEW TESTAMENT

Wise Men

> *And when they had come into the house, they saw the young Child with Mary His mother, and fell down and worshiped Him. And when they had OPENED THEIR TREASURES, THEY PRESENTED GIFTS TO HIM: GOLD, FRANKINCENSE, AND MYRRH. (Matthew 2:11) NKJV.*

To carry gold, frankincense and myrrh from a distant land to Bethlehem to worship Jesus was really a lot of sacrifice on their part. Upon arrival and seeing Jesus, they took to worship as a King and they presented their best gifts to Him.

Jesus

> *...we believe that Jesus died and rose again. (1 Thessalonians 4:14) NKJV.*

The Master who choose to die for his people; the man who lived to die to have all men back to God -surely, his love for his creation is awesome and amazing. No love surpasses this love. He gave himself as a perfect gift and sacrifice for the redemption of men.

Peter

> *He got into one of the boats, the one belonging to Simon, and asked him to put out a little from shore. Then he sat down and taught the people from the boat. (Luke 5:3) NIV.*

Once Jesus had a large crowd to preach to by the seaside, Peter offered his boat to Jesus to enable him to reach the masses.

Barnabas

> *Joseph, a Levite from Cyprus, whom the apostles called Barnabas (which means "son of encouragement"), sold a field he owned and brought the money and put it at the apostles' feet. (Acts 4: 36-37 NIV; addition mine).*

Of a truth, Barnabas was a son of encouragement. A man who will sell his land and give the proceeds to fund a Kingdom work.

Lydia

> *Now a certain woman named Lydia heard us. She was a seller of purple from the city of Thyatira, who worshiped God. The Lord opened her heart to heed the things spoken by Paul. (Acts 16:14) NKJV.*

Lydia did not only worship God with her mouth but also with her substance. She was also humble to listen to Apostle Paul teach her the ways of God. She did not pride herself with the money she had.

MODERN DAY

As I bring this chapter to a close, I want to make reference to a man in the 20th Century who made a tremendous contribution to society. He is the person of John D. Rockefeller. He had a lifestyle of making money and again by giving it back to society. From age sixteen (16) when he was contracted as Booking Clerk with Hewitt and Tuttle until he became the owner of

Standard Oil, it is a known fact that he kept a Red cover notebook known as "Ledger A" where he kept records of his giving to society.

Once delivering a message at Fifth Avenue Baptist on his 50th birthday on 26th September, he pinpointed from the notebook how he spent:

- » Very little on clothing.
- » Barely minimum on food.
- » Virtually nothing on personal amusement.
- » Hugely on charitable giving.

He remarked that "when I was only making a dollar, I was giving [away] five, ten or twenty five cents." His recorded gifts went to Baptist groups included the Five Points, the Mite Society, Foreign Missions and a poor woman in church and so forth.

Later as his resources multiplied, his charitable giving increased and he broadened his scope of giving. Those who benefitted from the widened scope of his philanthropic work were a Catholic orphanage, non-sectarian industrial school, Swedish mission and the University of Chicago. It is interesting to note that his first gift to University of Chicago was $600,000.00 and his last gift to the institution was $10 million. In all, his total giving to the school by December 1910 was $35million.

There was a phenomenon about this man in that he had his eyes darting around in church looking for the next needy person to help. Moreover, he had a daily habit of reviewing who to help at breakfast table with his family.

The Legacy // **chapter seventeen**

What a way to live! Let this man's story inspire you to also leave a good legacy behind.

There are many others who have come after Rockefeller who are doing incredibly well.

End Note

The Rockefeller Legacy | Excellence in Philanthropy
http://www.philantrophyroundtable.org/topic/excellence_in_ philanthropy/the _rockfeller_legacy

Conclusion

Before you finally put this book down, I want to kindly ask you this question: what will you be remembered for? Were you a giver or taker? The answer lies with you. You were born to be a contributor in your generation; so, take up the responsibility that goes with it.

For the poor will never cease from the land; therefore I command you, saying, 'You shall open your hand wide to your brother, to your poor and your needy, in your land.' (Deuteronomy 15:11) NKJV.

If the poor will never cease in the land, then the wealthy will not cease in the land as well. When a believer, like you and I, learns to walk through the land with open hands, many lives will be touched.

Be the open hand that feeds the poor. Be the open hand that reaches out to the orphans and widows. Be the open hand that touches the homeless. Be the open hand that touches people in the hospitals and prisons. I trust you will be the open hands in your generation. Stay blessed as you do so.

Frederick Osei-Manu

www.ingramcontent.com/pod-product-compliance
Lightning Source LLC
Chambersburg PA
CBHW031631210526
45464CB00004B/1848